SINGLING
A New Way to Live the Single Life

SINGLING

A New Way to Live the Single Life

John R. Landgraf

Westminster/John Knox Press
Louisville, Kentucky

Book design by Gene Harris

First edition

Published by Westminster/John Knox Press
Louisville, Kentucky

PRINTED IN THE UNITED STATES OF AMERICA

9 8 7 6 5 4 3 2 1

Library of Congress Cataloging-in-Publication Data

Landgraf, John R.
Singling, a new way to live the single life / John R. Landgraf. — 1st ed.
p. cm.
Includes bibliographical references.
ISBN 0-664-25086-6

1. Single people—United States—Religious life. I. Title.
BV4549.S5L35 1990
248.8'4—dc20 89-29308
CIP

For the many singlers

who gave me ideas;

for my New York and Oakland colleagues,

who gave me time to write them down;

and for Annie,

who gives me love

Contents

Prologue

Another book for single adults? No. In the midst of a society crowded with information about how to "score," this is not just another singles book. It is a leap of faith. It proposes an entirely new way to see and do the single life.

In an earlier book, *Creative Singlehood and Pastoral Care,*[1] I advanced the idea that singlehood today, including long-term or lifelong singlehood, is no longer an undesirable or abnormal way to live. On the contrary, I suggested, for many people it may be *the* identity and lifestyle that promises wellness, fulfillment, security, and "salvation" more than any other—including marriage, our most common form of coupling. In today's world, I argued, until a person experiences singlehood as her or his concert (not merely a prelude, interlude, or postlude), that person is not adequately equipped to sustain a healthy marriage anyway; "the prime requisite to being well-married to another person is being *well-married to oneself.*"[2] I buttressed my argument with statistics: for instance, that life expectancy in America has risen from 47 years at the turn of the century to 74 years and is still rising, forcing people either to develop the special skills required to sustain relationships over a very long period of time or to separate.

What I wrote several years ago is still valid, but it did not go far enough. Since then I have been shaped by responses to what I wrote—from readers, students, and workshop participants across the United States and Canada. The impassioned suggestions of these women and men encouraged me. They spurred me to think ever more expansively about the values of singlehood and the needs of single adults. My ideas about living the single life began to expand, even explode, and as I shared them people urged me to prepare a book on the topic I came to call "singling."

Singling embraces a new method and focus—an approach emphasizing the process by which one becomes healthily single, on the inside as well as on the outside. I am grateful to the many counseling clients, workshop participants, interview subjects, and friends who prodded me into this approach. I am convinced it is a helpful one, and I have done my best to set it forth clearly in an open-ended, inclusive, practical way.

Not only has my approach changed from that of my first book, my target audience has also changed. *Creative Singlehood* primarily addressed clergy and therapists who counsel with single adults. Only secondarily was that book aimed at single people themselves. However, hundreds of singles read it, and they provided my most enthusiastic and valuable feedback. Because of all they gave me, this present volume is my gift to them.

The many singling stories and case vignettes used in this book are real. I included them for reading enjoyment and learning value and to help singling pilgrims feel less lonesome. For privacy's sake I have changed people's names and some details.

Numerous people have helped with this project. To list them all would be impossible. I thank my friend Dick Bolles, who liked my original idea and helped me pursue it. I am indebted to Pamela Abbey, Heather Entrekin, Florence Fairhill, Warren Furnish, Anne Harroun, John Philip Landgraf, Marc LeSuer, Heidi Miguel, and David Wheeler, who read early drafts of the book and made helpful comments; and to Terry Burch, Carroll Wright, and Margaret Cowden for contributing substantial ideas. I applaud the encouragement of Becky Laird and Betty Erickson, who affirmed what I wrote when I wondered if I was on the right track. Patricia Dyck was a helpful resource as well. Most of all, I thank my skillful single friend Joan Thatcher for sharing her editorial expertise and enriching my ideas with hers as she helped me refine the manuscript, and Harold Twiss, my editor at Westminster/John Knox Press, for all he did to see the project through.

One last introductory thought. Because my approach is different from those of others who have written about singlehood, I encourage the non-single reader to read as if single. Approached from this minority perspective, the single experience may come alive for you in ways you otherwise might miss. As one woman put it in a recent workshop, "I came for one thing, and what I'm carrying away is something totally different." Then, seeing my puzzled look, she graciously added, "But it was well worth the trip."

J.R.L.

PART ONE

The Singling Way

1

The Case for Singling

Ellis was married for twelve years. The first six were good. The next six were not so good, although he learned more about himself during the not-so-good years than he had in the previous six. "Maybe that's progress," he kept telling himself. It wasn't. If anything, he regressed.

Then, following a divorce that simply had to happen for his sanity, Ellis had no mate at all for seven years. The first three were not so good. The next four were very good. This time Ellis learned more from the good years. "Maybe that's progress," he told himself. This time he was right.

Ellis grew to like being single. He learned to believe in singlehood, even in the necessity of becoming single on the road to maturity. He also came to believe, in a new way, in marriage, so much so that he married again, this time with eyes wide open.

But unlike the first time, this time Ellis married a truly single woman; and unlike the first time, this time he married as a truly single man.

I will explain this strange statement in a moment. First, having told you a bit about Ellis and his life, I must ask, What about you? You may be single because of divorce, like Ellis, or because of your spouse's death, or because of desertion, or delay, or some kind of default, or maybe by design. Actually, we shall see that singles do choose their singlehood, whether consciously or unconsciously. It is also possible to relinquish singlehood if that is one's goal, although once one is truly single, relinquishment is an odious option.

Ellis swears that neither he nor his new wife has given up singlehood. They speak of themselves as "married singles." They like it that way. When Ellis married before, at twenty-one, he was not single, nor was his bride. Their marriage was probably doomed from the start. The joining of two non-single people is not a good basis for a lasting marriage in the modern world. You see, the opposite of "single," as the word is used here, is not "married" but "non-single." In this sense, none of us is born single, any more than one is born married. Every one of us is born non-single.

To elaborate, no one expects a child to be single. Adolescent runaways try it, but they rarely bring it off because they are poorly equipped for singlehood. Successful singlehood means being a whole self. Such maturation takes time and is never accomplished in isolation or by a preemptive severing of one's roots. Becoming single is difficult. Most people, including adults, never make it.

This book is for people who want to *become* single.

Why write another book when there are already many books directed to the "singles market" that are well researched and useful? This book takes a unique approach in at least two ways.

First, in the current literature all nonmarried people are viewed as singles. In contrast, we shall see that *singlehood does not automatically accompany nonmarriage.* A person can have no spouse and still not be single.

Second, most other authors assume that all single persons have no mate. In contrast, we shall see that one can indeed have a husband, wife, live-in lover, "covenant partner," or other primary relationship *without renouncing one's singlehood.*

Singlehood Redefined

Some other things we shall discover in this book are:

- Singlehood can be a state of high-level wellness.
- One can be single and sexually whole.
- One can be well married to oneself.

- Once wholly single, a person is free to have a lifemate—or to not have one.
- Singlehood is always lived within relationships.

Singlehood is a way of life one must intentionally choose and ought never to stop choosing. This is something like learning a second language. It not only gives a person useful new ways to communicate, it also improves one's old ways of communicating. It refines one's original language. In the context of this book, your "original" language is the one you used before singling began, your "non-single" language.

By the way, to master a second language is to learn to think in the idioms of that language without translating from your original language. You will have mastered singlehood when you think in its idioms.

Nancy was one of my best teachers about singling. She came to seek my help following the failure of her fifth marriage. She was a sensitive, successful businesswoman burdened with a triple curse: brains, beauty, and wealth. By sheer coincidence our first meeting occurred on her thirty-ninth birthday.

Nancy told me that throughout her thirty-nine years she had never been without a man in her life (not "men" but *a* man) for more than a couple of months. Never. Initially it was her father, who incestuously violated her. Then it was her stepfather, who did the same. At age sixteen she eloped with a man twice her age, the father of her only child. He promptly abandoned her and their unborn baby the moment he learned she was pregnant. So much for marriage number one—and the second through the fifth were no better. Two of her ex-spouses were in prison, and her most recent husband was probably on his way there.

Nancy quickly formulated two goals for her therapy: (1) to overcome her powerful tendency to be drawn to "a sick man in need of rescue" and (2) to remain an unattached adult, by which she meant without any man in her life, for one full 365-day year. She put her goals in writing and gave me a photocopy. Happily, Nancy achieved both goals—and what a glorious celebration we had when she came to see me on her fortieth birthday! Soon after that I moved to another city and eventually lost track of her, but she followed through with an excellent therapist and the last I heard she had made it through a second full year. She was singling and well on her way toward singlehood.

If Nancy could do it, given her background and personality, so can you—if you want to.

This chapter identifies some key ideas and redefines some commonly abused terms that workshop participants have helped me clarify. These ideas are cornerstones on which one can begin to build a single life.

Just what is "singlehood"? And what is "singling"?

What Singlehood Means

This book takes a new approach to what singlehood is.

Singlehood is a state of existence, a way of being. It is a condition of encouraging, affirming, and maintaining one's integrity as a self. It is being willing—and learning how—to become increasingly self-aware, self-preserving, self-affirming, self-fulfilling, and autonomous (self-governing). It is taking responsibility for one's own well-being (total health and wholeness). It is making decisions for one's own life.

As I said at the start, the opposite of single is non-single. A person may never have married or may be formerly married and still not be single. But once a person is fully single, she or he will strongly tend to maintain singlehood no matter what—even if marriage comes, for example. And once single, one does not need to abandon singlehood to have a good marriage. Actually, the reverse is true: Good marriages can be made and sustained only by singles. People who only know how to be non-single cannot do it.

But, you may ask, doesn't this concept of being single equate with self-centeredness? Would it not eliminate being a giving person? Wouldn't it rule out all self-sacrificial acts of kindness? Isn't it saying no to everybody except yourself?

Not on your life. Singlehood, if it is a healthy, whole singlehood, is always lived within relationships; otherwise its value would be meaningless. We humans are relational beings. Thus singlehood implies a strong self-identity with a relational lifestyle. Wholeness as a single also means having the power to say yes when yes is called for, no when no is called for, and knowing when to say which—not just in sexual matters but in every aspect of interpersonal living. One has a choice as to one's response, for instance, to someone else's "But I love you!" or "You *will* give me just one more chance, won't you?"

People who are fully single are able to keep their own power intact while freely allowing others to keep theirs. They have "self-power awareness," and in embracing their autonomy they are able to function *inter*dependently without succumbing to those addictive dependencies that limit one's aliveness, love, and freedom.

Nora is such a single. She'd be the first to admit she doesn't have it all together—none of us is perfect—but as I see it she's pretty close, and although Nora is a modest person, I believe she knows what a grown-up single she is; she has a lot of self-power awareness. In a recent letter, she wrote:

> I am amazed how good life can be. It seems each year is sweeter than the year before. On my seventy-fifth birthday several hundred folk surprised me with the party of my life. Among the cards and gifts, they graced me with a silver-plated trowel in honor of my organic garden, which yielded its best harvest ever this year. I had a veritable cornucopia of vegetables to share with all my friends in the church and neighborhood.
>
> I don't understand adults of any age who are bored. My biggest problem has always been time management—too many wonderful things to do, too many marvelous people to do them with, and only 168 hours in the week!

Some forty years ago, Nora's husband took his own life. Nora has been a widow ever since. Among her many achievements she has taught school, completed a couple of postgraduate degrees, been dean of a college, and become the first woman in her denomination ordained to the ministry in her state. She is as fully alive and fully single as anyone I know. Nora is one of the reasons I know singling is a worthwhile enterprise.

What Singling Means

A main focus of this book is on the process of singling. The singling process is simply the way one gets to singlehood; one must travel the singling path to become single instead of non-single. Both non-single and single are identities, ways of self-definition. Non-single and single have little to do with legal documents or sacraments of the church; they have a lot to do with how one sees oneself and how one lives in the light of that perception.

First, then, *singling is the process of moving toward singlehood.* Another name for singling might be "singlework." I prefer singling, because the path to singlehood is not just work. The journey is playful too.

Second, *singling is needed because none of us was born single.* Singling is actually a fundamental task of life, since each of us began life not with singlehood but with connectedness—an extreme form of non-singleness. In childhood and early adolescence, we remained connected (non-single) with our mother and others on whom we depended for food, shelter, clothing, and love.

Out of our original connectedness must emerge the process of singling. Just as only a few special people purposely take the more difficult path in choosing a career, only a select few purposely seek singlehood. Jeremiah did it in the Old Testament, and Jesus in the New Testament. But you and I are neither Jesus nor Jeremiah. Most of us will think about singling or singlehood only when we have to because it feels as if we have no choice.

Even when it would appear that they had no other choice, I have seen people avoid beginning their singling as if they were avoiding the plague. Men are especially good at such avoidance, often remarrying as soon as possible after a divorce or the death of a spouse. I know a distinguished psychiatrist who has married four times. He has cleverly maintained non-single continuity with little more than a small inconvenience, a temporary interruption. In his defense, my psychiatrist friend is doubtless aware that many men who do not remarry literally sicken and die. The suicide rate for widowers remains woefully high, year after year. I suspect, however, that his fear of singlehood is stronger than his fear of death. It is as if some men would rather die than enter into the singling process.

I find that incredibly sad.

This book is for people on a voyage toward singlehood. It offers hope and practical suggestions about the singling voyage—about how to grow toward singlehood self-consciously, efficiently, effectively, and even comfortably.

Because clarity is important, I want to amplify our understanding of singlehood and singling before moving on.

What Singlehood and Singling Are Not

First, *singlehood is not a state defined by law.* It does not mean never having made it to the altar, nor does it mean having gone to the courthouse for a decree of divorce. Most people assume that the opposite of single is married. Not so. I repeat: The opposite of single is non-single.

Let me elaborate.

Today, a multitude of people are neither single nor married. Even if one uses the most menial definition—that marriage is nothing more than a formalized, institutionalized mating arrangement between a human male and a human female—a great number of non-single persons are also unmarried. There are those who are clearly mated but to persons of their same sex. There are our vast and growing company of elders, who often live and travel in pairs but avoid marriage for economic and legal reasons. There are the devoutly religious, such as nuns or monks, who voluntarily relinquish any claim to singleness to merge into tight-knit communities. There are our babies and children, who are neither married nor single as these terms are commonly used.

And then there are the myriad experiments and experimenters: couples who live together, do business together, co-own property, participate as partners in producing biological children or serving as foster parents; families who live communally with other families on co-op farms—and on and on it goes, all, typically, without benefit of religious or civil ceremony.

Are these all marrieds? Clearly not. Are they all singles, then? Again, clearly not. Just as one's name on a church roll does not necessarily mean one is a true Christian, one's social or institutional connection—or lack thereof—does not necessarily define one's true identity.

Some are singles. Some are not. Most could not articulate whether they are single or not and probably don't care—or at least they don't think about it.

So, are people either single or non-single, with the institution of marriage being simply the most common form of non-single living? Well, yes . . . and no. Like most things in life, it isn't all that clear-cut. Actually, people are more or less single or more or less non-single; that is, one finds oneself on a continuum that might be represented like this:

Non-Single —————————————————— Wholly Single

As you read on, then, ask yourself where you are on this continuum. Nancy saw herself way to the left. However, very few adults, unless severely disabled, are actually at the left end of our continuum. Most adults, for example, have developed some skills for independent decision-making and are quite capable of spending blocks of time by themselves. Such skills are singling skills.

But even among mature adults, relatively few will see themselves at the right end of the continuum either, unless they lie to themselves.

This brings me to a second idea as to what singlehood is not. Stated simply, *singlehood is not a static condition but a dynamic one.* People may be wholly single by law, as when one's divorce is final, but I have met precious few who are wholly single in fact. They are people in process. They are singles (legally) engaged in the process of singling (actually). To illustrate, let us amplify our continuum to look like this:

Non-Single		Slightly Single		Somewhat Single			Mostly Single		Wholly Single	
0	1	2	3	4	5	6	7	8	9	10

We might now admit that becoming wholly single—a perfect 10—may be realizable for some monks and mystics, but for most of us it remains a position which, at different times of life, we move toward, or embrace, move away from, or flee, or move against, or wrestle with.[1] The important thing is that we move, lest we stagnate.

To put it another way, *single describes a state of being, while singling describes a process.* The single's world is more that of the action verb than that of the static noun.

It is more dynamic and more accurate, then, to say, "I am Joanne, a singling person," than to say "I am Joanne, a single." A parallel construct to "a singling person" might be "a burning candle."

The reason this dynamic-rather-than-static concept matters so much is that none of us was born single. One becomes single or one doesn't, but singlehood never happens automatically. Melissa found this out.

Melissa was a handsome woman with beautiful silver hair and a winsome smile that almost balanced the sadness in her eyes. She was the last to introduce herself during the informal opening of a singles workshop I was conducting at a retreat center.

She began by saying, "John, I'm Melissa, and I don't think I've ever been single one day in my entire life!" She was very ill at ease about what she called "my single estate." She was very married—to her deceased husband! "With Jim gone," she said, "my life feels like an afterthought."

As it turned out, Melissa's self-assessment ("I don't think I've ever been single one day in my entire life") was accurate. Here is more of her story, as she shared it later:

> I grew up in a wonderful family—very strict and very religious, but also very loving. I was real close to my mom

> and dad and brothers and sisters. When I finally moved away from home, it was into a sorority house at a small college. My sorority sisters became a second family to me. Then, on the same day I got my baccalaureate degree, I also got my "M.R.S." degree: Jim and I got married on graduation day.
>
> I felt totally unprepared for marriage, but looking back I can see I knew more about marriage than I did about being single. I knew nothing about being single except that I was scared to death of it. Did you ever hear of "senior panic"? Well, I had it. Graduating and going out into the world without a husband was a curse worse than death! I remember feeling so sorry for a sorority sister who had to do that.
>
> Now look at me. It's twenty-five years later and here I am, having to do exactly what my sorority sister had to do, and I'm no more prepared for it now than I was then. No, I'm probably even less prepared for it now. Then at least I had a brand-new degree and some hot skills to sell.

Melissa's story is not unusual. Many women and men have shared similar tales (the male versions differ only in detail) to explain that they are more comfortable with being non-single than with singlehood. Understandably, then, the singling process is uncomfortable too, since it is an "unnatural" process of moving toward an unknown, unfamiliar, and even scary new way of life. It is a process that may even be ridiculed by one's family or personal and professional peers, because the singling person is marching to the beat of a different drummer than they are.

To you who are dreading the unknown world of singlehood, I say, I wish I could reduce your fears. Unfortunately, I cannot; but maybe I can at least awaken a hope or two.

Many people have discovered that singling is a good thing to do and that wholly single is a good way to be, even—dare I say it?—a great way to be. It does not mean one has no friends, or no lover, or no spouse (in the present or past). Melissa could become as single as she wished without dishonoring her long and happy marriage.

One more introductory thought. The media in our pop culture

are constantly sending us signals that being non-single is normal while being single is abnormal. Advertising of all kinds—TV, radio, films, and music—bombards us with "togetherness" messages night and day. This renders singling doubly difficult. Beware. Begin to pay attention to what you watch and hear. Begin to look and listen critically.

At a workshop, all of us were engaged in an assignment involving a time of silent personal reflection. Suddenly, a man I'll call Pete shouted full voice, "Damn it, I hate being single!" Right on target, Pete. So do we all, at first. We all were born to embrace our non-single estate and abhor singlehood. Of course, we all were born dependent children, too. But some of us have become doggedly determined to grow up to full maturity, whatever it means and whatever the cost.

Singling is about that pilgrimage—the one we start when reality hits and we can do no other.

2

When Reality Hits

Virginia and Ray, a couple I know, recently celebrated their fifty-fifth wedding anniversary. They'd be the first to admit it hasn't all been a bed of roses, but their marriage has been good and still is. They met as children, and their long courtship has carried them all the way through grade school, high school, and college; to the altar; and through the decades since. Now in their seventies, they treasure their family and memories. Neither of them has ever been single in any sense except that they weren't born married. I'm quite sure they don't think about it or care. Why should they? They've enjoyed a rich life, they remain happy now, and, as the saying goes, "If it ain't broke, don't fix it."

"Some people have it made," as another saying goes.

For most of us, though, life has been neither as simple nor as kind as it has to Virginia and Ray. Fate has intervened to force us to face realities we would truly rather have lived without.

In contrast to Ray and Virginia, meet three singling people forced to face their particular realities.

Harold, a struggling widower, entered a large bookstore to look for a couple of recommended books. After browsing randomly in sections labeled Women's Studies, Marriage and Family, Psychology, Sociology, Sexuality, Self-Help, and Gay and Lesbian Studies, he decided to ask for help. "Where are your singles books located?" he said hopefully. "Oh, we don't have a section for those," replied the store manager. "They're just mixed in wherever we can find a place for them."

Singling is facing the reality of feeling one has no place of one's own.

Celia, whose husband had divorced her, told her mother she had joined the singles group at her church. Her mother, with an irritated look on her face, snapped, "Well, I certainly hope you don't mingle with that bunch of neurotic leftovers too long," and then added as an afterthought, "Your job now, young lady, is to quit feeling sorry for yourself, make yourself as presentable as possible, and go out there and find some nice man to marry you—somebody a whole lot better than that bozo who saddled you with three kids and then ran out on you!"

Singling is facing the reality of judgment and pressure from significant others.

Helga, as she introduced herself at a workshop called "Learning to Live the Single Life," made no bones about her situation. "Here I am, forty-seven years old and single for the very first time," was the way she put it. She explained that she was the only child of immigrant parents who met and married in midlife. Her mother died when Helga was twelve. For the next five years she kept house for her father. When her father remarried, Helga soon eloped (at age seventeen). The man she married, himself an immigrant, was twenty years her senior. He adored Helga, was a marvelous provider, and, she hastened to add, left her well off financially. Tearfully, she told us her "darling Otto" had recently died of a massive cerebral hemorrhage. Ironically, he died the very day of their thirtieth wedding anniversary.

Helga said she came to the workshop "to learn how to go on living with no man to take care of, because I think I am too old to find another one. Now," said Helga, "I need to learn how to be single."

Singling is facing loss and starting over.

Folks like Harold, Celia, and Helga have helped me become an unabashed evangelist for singles' liberation.

In an age when we are witnessing at least some of the possibilities of children's liberation, black, brown, red, and yellow people's liberation, gray liberation, gay liberation, and certainly women's liberation, we have not yet seen much freeing change for the sixty million adults (in the United States alone) whom sociologists and other researchers usually refer to as "singles." The oppressive stereotyping of this numerically impressive minority continues virtually unabated, with the result that even singles themselves tend to think of these millions of people as abnormal—"leftovers," as Celia's mother put it, has-beens, or failures. Or, if we think of life as a concert, here are the poor lost souls admitted only to their bleak preludes, interludes, or postludes while the orchestra plays its symphony for the married folk and other non-single people skilled enough or lucky enough to be in coupled relationships.

Further, in most singles' imaginations the happy concertgoers all have idyllic marriages. That really is the best kind of life, they think to themselves. But if, alas, such is not to be my lot, they muse, how about second best? Or if not second best, how about third best? After all, any coupled relationship is better than none, isn't it?

No, it isn't. Ask Celia. Or Harold. Or Helga. I'd bet they know.

Actually, I think I know too. I was a lifelong non-single person, like Helga. I didn't elope at seventeen (although I considered it), but I exchanged my parents' nest for the comfortable nest of college life and then saw to it that graduation was accompanied by marriage at twenty-one. About seven years later the marriage died, and although we didn't get around to burying it for another seven years, I gradually and painfully began to realize that I had never been single. I needed to learn how to *become* single.

My trek toward singlehood began in the late 1960s. I am a slow learner. My journey took a long time.

Now, since 1975, I have been privileged to counsel and teach singles, and also therapists and clergy who deal with singles. I have met many Harolds, Helgas, and Celias along the way. They have helped me as much as I have helped them.

A "Reality Practice" Exercise

This is a simulation. It may help you get in touch (or back in touch) with what it feels like to be confronted with the reality of impending singlehood. If you wish, take a few minutes to do this exercise now. Use a separate piece of paper.

An Inductive Introduction to Singlehood

Find a quiet, comfortable space where you can be alone. Try to clear your mind and relax. Allow yourself to center down and become self-aware. You may want to close your eyes for a few minutes. When you are ready:

> Imagine yourself in the waiting room of a hospital ICU (Intensive Care Unit). You are sitting alone. In the ICU, in critical condition, is the most important person in your present life. More than a best friend, this is your soulmate, lover, playmate, companion—your primary person. This dear one just experienced a severe heart attack and was brought here by ambulance. Right now, the coronary thrombosis has been arrested, and your love is resting with the help of the hospital's life support systems. You don't know whether death is at hand or not, but it is highly possible. As a matter of fact, what the physician said, exactly, was, "You'd better prepare yourself for the worst."

Take a few minutes to write what you can of your thoughts and feelings. *Note:* If you have difficulty getting into this situation, close your eyes and let your imagination run free for a while. You might think about your hopes for this relationship. Maybe, for instance, the intimacy and fit between you and this person is the best you have ever known. You realize you are heavily invested in the relationship. You've thought, This is the one I'd like to grow old with. And now . . . death, years and years ahead of time? Try writing what you can.

If the exercise becomes unbearably uncomfortable for you, stop. Take a few more minutes just to relax and let your mind wander. Now try to write what you are feeling about all this and why.

When you have finished, take time to ponder the simulated situation and your feelings about it. No two people react exactly the same way. Here are some questions to ask yourself:

1. How do I typically deal with crisis?
2. How well do I handle losses?
3. Would I seek help? Of whom?

4. How would I heal my memories?
5. What if I never again meet anyone with whom I want to spend my life?

Why face reality? Singlehood is almost never chosen—at least initially. If we are to have it, it chooses us. Reality hits us suddenly, or dawns upon us gradually, and then we face it . . . maybe.

We humans rarely seek major identity changes. We are more apt to heed the insistent push of pain than the gentle pull of growth. It is usually pain that forces the adult whose non-single identity and lifestyle are no longer viable—forces her or him either to escape into the world of fantasy or to begin the process of singling. The pain is one's inner voice saying, "I've got to learn how to do this!" or "I've got to become single now that I am!" or some such imperative.

It may help to write your personal imperative, in your own words, on a piece of paper. Carry it in your pocket or purse, or use it as a bookmark.

All relationships end. Even the most securely mated person in the world may need singling skills at a moment's notice. This is because all relationships end in separations. Consider Virginia and Ray, the couple at the beginning of this chapter. Unless they die simultaneously, as in a plane crash, sooner or later one of them will enter the portal of singling by the death of the other.

If the widow or widower refuses to become single, which is entirely possible, she or he can continue a non-single identity by retreating into the past and essentially living in the world of fantasy. To do so is to deny reality and avoid a fresh future. The choice is always ours, and the choice is always made. As the adage has it, "Not to decide is to decide."

All relationships end in separations. Always.

Besides living as if the separation had never happened, there are three other ways to forever avoid singling: (1) Become a hermit, a recluse, and live in total seclusion—a hard thing for a non-single person to do, although I know some widows and widowers who have done it; (2) never, ever, enter into a relationship—not even a friendship—except on the most superficial level possible, revealing nothing of yourself that matters at all; or, (3) take your own life in suicide before anyone you care about has a chance to hurt you or die on you.

Let me clearly state that I do not recommend any of these strategies. They are far too expensive.

What I do recommend, instead, is that we each learn how to survive the ending of relationships. Singling is about surviving endings and making fresh beginnings.

Beginning Singling

There are certain basic entryways people take to start on their singling paths. The next several chapters contain stories and discussions that illuminate the various entryways, or at least the main ones:

- Singling because of death
- Singling because of divorce
- Singling because of delay
- Singling by design

Chances are that you will recognize yourself in several of the singling stories that created these chapters. It may be tempting to focus only on those with which you readily identify. I encourage you to look at them all, however.

Why?

First, each scenario has been included because it is instructive. It conveys principles and guidelines about singling that will be useful to you no matter who you are.

Second, you may actually find yourself on the threshold of several different portals. Most people do. The title of a given chapter is more a clue to its context than a description of its contents.

Third, it is important to ask yourself, again and again, "What do I believe about singlehood?"

A famous writer about holistic health, Norman Cousins,[1] explains why believing is so important. He points out that while medical science has identified the primary systems of the human body (circulatory system, digestive system, endocrine system, autonomic nervous system, parasympathetic nervous system, and immune system), two other systems are central in the proper functioning of a human being. They are the healing system and the belief system.

Cousins says the two work hand in hand. The healing system is the way one mobilizes all his or her resources to combat disease, and the belief system activates the healing system. The belief system represents the unique element in human beings that makes it possible for the human mind to affect the workings of the body and spirit. What one believes about one's problems has a great deal to do with the way one functions. For instance, one's confidence, or lack of it, in the prospects of recovery from serious illness affects the chemistry of the body. One's belief system can convert the will to live into a plus factor in any contest of forces involving disease. Cousins hastens to add that the belief system cannot be substituted for competent medical attention in serious illness; both are essential. The belief system is not just a state of mind, he insists. It is a prime physiological reality. It is the application of options to the maintenance of health and the fight against disease. It is the master switch that gets the most out of whatever is possible. What one believes is the most powerful option one has.

Returning to our discussion of getting started in singling, let's say you believe, as most people do, that singlehood is equivalent to a disease, and therefore you remain ill at ease with your singlehood. What will you do? Probably, you will muster all available forces to fight it and annihilate or cure it.

But singlehood is not a disease; it is a state of high-level wellness. Therefore, to "cure" or "fix" it is the wrong thing to do! If you succeed in healing the so-called disease of singlehood, you are actually avoiding or evading a condition that should be pursued, welcomed, and befriended.

To put it another way, if you "cure" your singlehood you will merely put off facing it until another day, because sooner or later it will be yours to face unless you die a sudden or premature death.

And if you try to cure it but do not succeed? Then, the best you can expect, whether you ever marry or not, whether you live with others or by yourself, is to continue living in the manner to which you were born: as a non-single person in your mind and heart.

At a singles conference, a well-dressed older woman watched attentively as I put my SINGLING BY DEATH—DIVORCE—DELAY—DESIGN outline on the chalkboard. By the time I finished, her hand was in the air. "Now let me see if I understand this business," she began. "I've been through singling by divorce, then by death, then by delay, then by divorce again, and now by death again. Maybe it's time for me to get started on singling by design. Do you think so?"

Yes—and how!

PART TWO

Entryways

3

Singling Because of Death

In a sense, singling by death may be the least complicated entryway to singlehood.[1] While not the easiest to achieve, it is the easiest path toward singlehood to acknowledge as real. Widows and widowers know that, in society's eyes at least, they are now single, and they say so, as Julie does below.

> I lost my husband last January.
>
> I think he kept himself alive through the holidays by sheer willpower. He always had lots of willpower. But finally his will to die got stronger than his will to live. I don't blame him. Who could? He'd suffered plenty. He'd spent most of the money he worked so hard to save so the kids could have a better education than he had—spent it all on that damn cancer. He got to the point where he couldn't stand being a burden anymore. He used to say over and over, "I'm just one big management problem."
>
> Now he's no trouble at all.
>
> But then who am I kidding? That's not true. Of course he's still trouble. It's just a different kind of trouble. Now the trouble is right here. The trouble is with me. Now it's Julie's problem.
>
> You'd think, after all those months of awful sickness, almost a whole year's worth . . . and after living without him for almost another whole year . . . that I'd be over it. But

I know I'm not. That man is still in my head and heart and soul.

Damn. When am I going to be over it?

Julie had a lot going for her. Both of her children were grown—the younger in college and the older one living independently. She had a master's degree and a secure job as a high school teacher. Her twenty-four-year marriage had been a satisfying one. "Better than most," Julie told herself. Oh, Geoff had worked too hard, by his own admission. He called himself a workaholic. But as Geoff himself had exclaimed, "Who in the name of heaven could have predicted pancreatic cancer?" What could he have done to avoid that? He had never been in the hospital in his life except to be born. Who could have imagined that Julie and Geoff would never see their silver anniversary?

Losing one's lifemate by death is an excruciating and traumatic experience, especially if death comes unexpectedly or in an undignified manner. However, death has a final ring to it, and such a finality can help render the process of singling clear and clean. "I was a married woman for as long as I can remember," a widow said to her minister, "and now that book is closed." Once she was married; now she is not. What happened, for all its pain, is clear: her spouse died. It is sad, but it cannot be changed. Her new life situation is an unmistakable, irreversible fact. Her state is thus an honorable one in terms of social attitudes and values. Everybody sympathizes with her.[2]

The very honorableness of a widow's or widower's situation, however, contains the seeds of delayed or unhealthy adaptation. Later in this chapter we will consider the possibility of Julie's remaining married to Geoff even though he is physically dead. First, let us consider the steps Julie needs to take in order to begin singling in a healthy way.

It is also important for divorced or deserted persons to understand the following process. While their circumstances may be different, the first steps they must take are essentially the same.

Good Grief

If a friend of yours lost a spouse in a train wreck and if, following that tragedy, your friend was not upset, what would you think? At first, you might wonder at such incredible composure. Then, if the composure continued for long, you'd probably begin to worry about *de*composure—about your friend's emotional health. And well you might, for according to all authorities in the field of death and dying (thanatology), it is normal to be upset when a loved one dies.

The upset may not be apparent during the shock stage, but it is there all the same. Centuries ago Jeremiah, a single man and prophet of Israel, wailed, "My anguish, my anguish! I writhe in pain! Oh, the walls of my heart!" (Jer. 4:19). Jeremiah's pain felt terminal at that moment, like life dying, but his behavior and lament were normal, given his circumstances.

I have met singles who felt like Jeremiah. Some of them were brave enough to join a "grief growth group" or attend a singles workshop. In the face of heartrending grief, strong emotions are completely appropriate. It is healthy for bereaved persons to experience themselves as heartsick, mentally numb, spiritually bleeding, and physically wiped out when they have been forced to begin singling as a byproduct of death.

Grief can be a good thing. It is surely a necessary thing. Grief work appropriately accomplished is good grief.[3] It is also good singling.

The term "grief" comes from a Latin word meaning "heaviness of spirit." There are different kinds of grief, but grieving always involves suffering, feelings of failure and lostness, and downright anguish. Experts have identified in healthy adults at least seven dynamics characteristic of the normal grieving process:

SHOCK
CATHARSIS
DEPRESSION
GUILT
PREOCCUPATION WITH LOSS

ANGER
and finally
RECOVERY.[4]

A little later in this chapter we will discuss these dynamics in some detail. Right now I want to emphasize that the hallmark of a good grief process is adequate recovery from the loss that triggered the grief.

The Three-Year Rule

Julie was being far too harsh with herself when she thought she should be "over it" in a year. After loss of a spouse, the grief process usually takes three to five years in a healthy adult. Three to five years! Ministers and mental health professionals are all familiar with persons for whom it has taken much longer—but rarely less than three years. Whether people are singling by death, desertion, or divorce, three years is usually the minimum recovery period.

Many singles want to argue against the three-year rule. They are quick to point out obvious exceptions—situations where a spouse's dying process spanned many years, or where the loss occurred on a couple's honeymoon after a whirlwind courtship so that the bereaved spouse hardly knew the new mate before death came, or where two old friends married within a few months following the deaths of both of their respective spouses, and the new marriage is doing just fine.

Fair enough. But the vehement resistance encountered whenever the three-year rule is mentioned simply verifies its validity. It is a guideline, not an absolute, and one is wise to presume in its favor.

Certainly there are exceptions. Shortly after my uncle Carl's death, my aunt Sarah wed her former employer and longtime friend, a never-married man. That was many years ago; they are still happily together. But the point is not changed because of such exceptions. The burden of proof is on the singling adult who would justify any exception to the three-year rule.

It is because of the three-year rule that widows and widowers or divorced or abandoned persons who quickly find another partner should consider that they may be "mating on the rebound," a perilous risk usually taken by very non-single people desperate to stay that way.

To do good grieving is simply to grieve wisely and well—effectively, efficiently, and as long as needed but no longer. Yes, I have seen someone like my friend Julie or my aunt Sarah arrive at a place of full recovery in less than three years—but not a lot less than three years, and less only because the mourner has done effective, efficient grieving: good grief.

Help for Your Grief

The three grieving years may be the best possible time to take your singling self into some pastoral counseling, spiritual direction, or psychotherapy. Part Three of this book can help you determine whether this is your need, and chapter 11, "Where to Find Help," contains specific suggestions for finding an appropriate helper.

If counseling is not available to you or you do not feel ready for it yet, here are three assignments I have given to counselees singling because of death. In some instances these suggestions are made one at a time over a period of months. In other instances, in the face of blocked grief, I have recommended all three at once.

1. Go grieve. Whatever wants to happen within you, let it happen. Let it happen now. Let it happen as much as it wants to. Don't ignore it. Don't fight it. Set aside time for it—perhaps both morning and evening time—each day. Especially in the earlier stages of your grieving process, cry as much as possible. Once the initial shock begins to give way, tears can help a lot. Catharsis (release) is natural, normal, useful. Let it come. Give yourself permission: "This is my daily appointment with me, my time to go grieve." Like the discipline involved in prayer and spiritual formation, consistent daily attention to grieving can only help.

2. Release your mate. Let your mate go. Don't try to keep yourself tied to your spouse, or your spouse to you, in any way. As it becomes possible, donate the personal wardrobe and other belongings to a charity so they can be used by needy people. When you are ready, bid a fond farewell to the nesting place you both called home and move to a nest all your own, a nest you feather for just your singling self.[5] Do not avoid the pain of singling by escaping into the home of a daughter, son, friend, or relative. Cherish your fond memories, but don't cling to your mate as a person or to the life you had together.

There are people whose non-singleness is their most prized asset. They prize it so much that if their spouses die (or leave them), they refuse to let go. They fear losing their identity as a husband or wife so desperately that, long after the fact, they cling steadfastly to dashed hopes and lost dreams in almost morbid fashion, like hanging on to a dead horse that can no longer be ridden.

This seems to happen most often when a spouse (let's make it a woman, though it could just as well be a man) has submerged her own identity in that of her mate. She has come to identify herself, in our imagined situation, as "Mrs. John Q. Jones, M.D., F.A.C.S."—the surgeon's wife. She may wistfully remember her life as "the former Sally Smith," a full-time teacher and part-time tutor of disabled children, who worked for many years to help her husband complete his training and establish his practice. But, if her husband dies, who is this woman who spent so many years as "Mrs. Doctor"? Who is she now? This often becomes an identity issue of such magnitude that seeking help from a professional therapist is a wise move.

Returning to the assignment of releasing your mate, ask yourself, "What are the advantages of embracing a relationship no longer available to me?" "What are the disadvantages of letting go of that which is gone?"

A therapist I know has a sign in the room where she conducts group therapy for grieving singles:

THE DEATH OF YOUR RELATIONSHIP
OCCURS WHEN YOU GIVE UP HOPE
OF REGAINING WHAT YOU HAVE LOST.

There is a time to let go.

3. Think single. To think, speak, and act single may feel awkward, strange, even phony. In order for it to feel authentic it needs the learning, risking, relearning, trying again, and practice that the entire singling process implies. This takes time and energy and you will make mistakes, many mistakes, if you are like most of us. However, to become single one must begin singling.

So start today. The task is learning to provide for yourself what was formerly provided by your mate. This means taking inventory of your internal and external resources and putting them to use. It means learning to be your own best friend. It means, little by little, becoming "well married" to yourself.

The how-tos will get easier and more obvious as you acquire more singling skills. Right now it is time to begin to step out on faith, however gingerly, daring to "act as if" you are single. It is a challenge and a goal. And it can be fun once the awkwardness lessens. In this sense singling is like skiing or dancing—hard work at first, but a lot of fun once you know the basics and are less fearful about falling on your face or looking like a clumsy dolt.

Bad Grief

If there is good grief, there is also bad grief.

When, at sixty-six years of age, Emily married Fred, her friends remarked that she was the luckiest woman alive. Fred was a rare find: handsome and wealthy, a gentleman and a churchman. He appeared younger than his seventy years, although his first wife's surgery, radiation treatments, chemotherapy, and lengthy terminal illness "wore me down to a frazzle," in Fred's words.

Emily had been a widow for seven years and had long since become quite single, and happily so. "You know one of the things I like best about you? You don't seem desperate to find a husband," said Fred on their first date.

When Fred asked Emily to marry him a couple of weeks later on their third date, she hesitated momentarily but then said yes.

Fred convinced her that because of his wife's long illness everybody would understand "as long as we aren't in too big of a hurry." The wedding took place a hundred days after the funeral.

When I met Emily several months later, she was obviously miserable. She told me some of her story and then, after some minutes of tearful silence, came to the heart of the matter through her tears:

> The trouble started as soon as we got back from our honeymoon. First came the recipes. Fred handed me her recipe box and asked me to use it! Next it was her wardrobe. Unfortunately, I'm the same size. He couldn't understand why I wouldn't want to wear her mink coat or an evening dress that cost a fortune and was only worn once. When I refused, he went into a grand pout and stopped talking to me for several days!
>
> Then there are the daily trips to the cemetery. At first he went alone, but now he insists I go with him to keep him company. I thought he'd give it up pretty soon, or make his visits shorter if I went along. I swear it's gone the other way; sometimes he stays at her grave for an hour!
>
> But the final blow has been that lately he calls me by her name every time we make love.

The problem was: Fred had not done his grief work. Fred was also a very non-single person. He was still emotionally married to his first wife, and now he had seriously compounded his grief problem by marrying Emily (which, I suspect, may have begun to feel like unfaithfulness or bigamy!). His psyche was trying to accomplish its grief work now (thus the visits to the cemetery), but it was all mixed up with guilt, depression, anger, and who knows what else—and here was Emily, caught in the unpredictable, crazy labyrinth of Fred's bad grief.

Bad grief is simply grief work not yet done—unresolved grief, blocked grief, grief avoided. Bad grief can lead to years or even a lifetime of stalemate, the griever remaining in a quagmire, stuck in some stage of the process and unready for the renewal and rebirth of singling.

The Dynamics of Grief

In this context we return to the seven dynamics of the grieving process mentioned earlier. Not everyone experiences all seven, and they do not necessarily follow one another in a neat order. They make up a seven-step path on the singling journey to wholeness—the path most singles must follow, normally taking three years or more, although some may traverse a six-step or five-step path and still do good grief.

1. Shock. The shock dynamic is nearly always first. It is typical of early grief crisis. Newly singling people feel numb. Sometimes they speak of what is happening as if it surely must be happening to somebody else. They may say, "This is unreal" or "I don't believe this is happening." A man whose wife drowned said, "The whole scene is just like watching a horror movie . . . only I'm in it!" It is a time when one musters the raw energy to "go through the motions" without fully facing the reality . . . yet.

2. Catharsis. While you are in grief you will tend to move in and out of shock, catharsis, depression, and anger. It is appropriate to list catharsis as the dynamic following shock, however, because it is often experienced next.

One definition of catharsis is the bringing to consciousness of our repressed ideas and feelings. (A simpler term might be "release.") "Repressed" in this context simply means "held back." Catharsis is experienced, sometimes gradually and sometimes suddenly, as a surge of feeling, a rush of emotion. There may be tears—inner tears or outer, visible tears. The latter are more effective because they are overtly released rather than suppressed.

For a person singling because of death, catharsis is the venting of everything pent up during the dying and since the death of one's partner. It usually occurs, stops, and then recurs, over and over again. But when the catharsis has run its course, it releases the mourning person and relief is felt. Sometimes one feels as if the crying will go on forever. Remember: It won't. When you are ready, your tears of grief will give you up.

3. Depression. One man could not understand why he felt so blue every time he came home to an empty house. After all, his wife of thirty-five years had died almost six months ago! We Americans are efficiency experts and pain avoiders. We want pain to stay away from us, and if it refuses to do so, then we want it to go away as fast as possible. That is too bad, because pain, honestly and fully expressed, can be a freeing experience.

Depression is a heavy word—a loaded term, because few persons want to think of themselves as depressed. But it is an accurate word. Following the loss of one's mate it is normal somewhere along the singling path to arrive at a place of acute depression. It usually happens after shock and catharsis, several weeks or months along. Like catharsis, it may come and go as if it had a will of its own. Grieving singles speak of bouts with depression or waves of depression.

Depression is the most dangerous dynamic on the grief road. Its dangers include lowered resistance to disease; running away from reality, perhaps by frantically escaping into one's work; and turning the depressive feelings in on oneself.

The experts feel that unexpressed anger turned inward underlies much depression. It is during these times that widows or widowers or divorced persons make themselves sick or even renounce their own lives. Some renounce life literally, in suicide.

Others in this painful condition go to the other extreme; they rush into a whirl of social activities and even remarry! A psychologist friend likens this kind of depression to a swimmer in trouble: struggling is apt to result in drowning, while relaxing and allowing the body to respond naturally will result in automatic surfacing.

Remember: The depressive feelings are normal and healthy, but feeding and watering them with self-pity or self-blame is not. If you feel stuck here, find a friend who has been through a loss similar to yours, or find a therapist.

4. Guilt. Guilt, like depression, can be elusive. It can come repeatedly . . . or hardly at all. It can strike at various points along the path (often during times of catharsis). It can take various forms:

> I feel just terrible about the way I neglected my wife. If only I'd known she'd be with me only for eight years and then be gone, I would never have put in so much overtime.
>
> To think that the last thing I ever said to him was nasty, just plain nasty. I don't think I can ever forgive myself for that.
>
> I know what the doctor said—that he had a heart attack. But I know what really happened; I drove him until he finally worked himself to death. More, more, more . . . big me, always wanting more!

Whatever shape the guilt takes, it needs to be acknowledged and faced head-on. The most efficient way to do that may be in a counseling relationship—with your minister, priest, rabbi, or therapist. A small warning: There is a distinction between appropriate guilt and neurotic or unhealthy guilt,[6] and the singling person sometimes has trouble knowing which is which. In a nutshell, appropriate guilt is that sense of contrition and remorse that has a basis in reality: "I feel guilty because I *am* guilty; I did wrong, and here's how I know it was wrong." Neurotic guilt is the product of fear of rejection or punishment. It is not rooted in reality—except the reality of one's inner conflicts.

If you have a history of feeling guilty "at the drop of a hat" and you've now lost your spouse by death, desertion, or divorce, talk with your minister or rabbi, personal physician, or someone else whose judgment you trust. If a referral for counseling is the result, muster your courage and go. I have seen unresolved guilt block many a singling process, sometimes for years and years.

5. Preoccupation with the loss. Julie could have remained married, in her heart, to her deceased husband, but she did not do so. However, Mary did. Several years after Brett's death she still wore black, refused to socialize, sat alone in the same church pew she and Brett shared for so many years, and always introduced herself as "Mrs. Brett Smith." She continued to live in the Smith house, which she refused to redecorate because she and Brett had chosen the wallpaper together. On special occasions she made a festive meal which she ate ceremoniously by herself with Brett's portrait across from her on his empty plate.

Mary had no history of mental illness and did not appear mentally ill now. All her adult life she had been known as a refined, cultured woman who was active in church and community affairs, and she still continued to dispatch her responsibilities dutifully.

Now, however, her most cherished activity was wistfully recounting the life she and Brett had shared together. Again and again, friends encouraged her to begin a new life as a single person, but she objected that "Brett wouldn't approve." Finally the friends gave up and left Mary to her rudderless, reclusive drifting.

There is an important difference between cherishing fond memories and becoming preoccupied with one's loss. Sometimes, however, the distinction becomes blurred, a fuzzy boundary between reality and fantasy. Fortunately, our memories do heal, and as they heal they become wonderfully selective. As the scripture says, we are fearfully and wonderfully made.[7] We remember that balmy summer night we left a party early to make love on an isolated moonlit beach. We conveniently forget the embarrassing night when we left another party early because our spouse drank too much champagne and embarrassed us.

If you are preoccupied with your lost love, you may be a grieving single suffering from guilt, or a misdirected sense of loyalty, or a false view of marriage as "forever" (in this life and in the next), or a fear of new relationships, or a fear of becoming truly single. There are many possibilities.

You need to grant yourself permission to let go—but you probably know that already, and find it an insurmountable hurdle. If so, do yourself a kindness. Seek a gentle but firm boost over that hurdle. For Arlene, a counseling interview with her minister provided such a boost:

PASTOR: As your minister and Paul's friend as well as yours, I think it's time for you to begin a new life, without Paul.

ARLENE: You really think he'd approve if I stopped acting like a widow?

PASTOR: Arlene, I think he'd be pleased. Furthermore, I think God would like to see you happier, and having some fun.

ARLENE: I don't know—I have to admit I've thought about it. I guess the truth is I'm sort of scared to venture out into the world of relationships after being married to Paul for so many years.

PASTOR: I appreciate your sharing that fear with me. I want you to know that once you begin that venture, I'll be glad to listen to how it's going for you, anytime, if you think that would help.

ARLENE: Thanks. It helps to know someone cares.

PASTOR: I do care . . . and I do hope you find life after Paul.

ARLENE: Maybe I can.

6. Anger. Anger is a powerful emotion in human life. Its force can be negative and destructive, but it can just as readily be positive and constructive. Often anger is a singling person's good friend, as when it recognizes one's innate worthfulness and demands that abuse or neglect stop.

Chapter 7, "Anger and Singling," deals with this topic in depth. Right now it is important to say: When anger appears in the grieving process, don't avoid it. Welcome it.

Elizabeth came to her counseling session furious.

ELIZABETH: As I left work to come over here this afternoon I realized I've been seeing you for a year, and then all of a sudden, just driving here in the car, I got mad. I mean, I just got madder and madder.

THERAPIST: Tell me a little more.

ELIZABETH: Well, Joey was gone seven months before I first came for counseling. That means it's been more than a year and a half since his death. Do you know that I still do not have any financial settlement of Joey's estate? I've changed lawyers, and the one I have now is terrific. I know she's doing all she can to expedite things. But that damn Joey! He knew full well the will he'd done in Michigan wouldn't "fly" in California. (*Pause; then, sarcastically*) Of course, we'd only lived in California eleven years when he died. But every time I'd mention it he'd say, "Don't nag me, don't nag me. I'll get around to it one of these days, and I'll do it a lot faster if you get off my back." (*Pause*) I swear, I didn't nag him. The last four years of his life I never even brought it up. Oooh, I could just kill him! (*Laughter*) Oops, what did I just say?

THERAPIST: (*Laughs*) I think you said a mouthful. Congratulations!

ELIZABETH: Congratulations? For what?

THERAPIST: This is the first time I've ever seen you angry.

ELIZABETH: Oh, I get angry. I get angry a lot. Just never at Joey. Until today. Today I just couldn't help it. I'm outraged.

THERAPIST: I'm pleased. This is a sign that your grieving is coming along nicely.

Anger is the emotional lifeblood of the grieving singler, a definite "plus sign" on the road to recovery, and often also a help in resolving any leftover depression. There comes a time when most mourners do get angry, whether the reasons for the anger are clear or not. Good news: Such angry feelings are natural and normal, as Elizabeth learned. Bad news: They may be handled in inappropriate ways. It would have been inappropriate, for example, for Elizabeth to misdirect her anger from its real target, Joey, by turning it inward and retreating into guilt or depression, or by turning it outward against some other person.

During this "rage stage" you may be angry at yourself for failing to do or say all you wanted before the final separation. You may be angry at the medical professionals for what they did or didn't do. You may be angry at your clergyperson for being of so little help, or at God for the same reason. Or, like Elizabeth, you may be angry at your long-gone mate.

Whatever the cause of the anger, be careful not to suppress

it. Admit it, befriend it by welcoming it, express it, and examine the issues that spawned it. It is these *issues* that beg resolution.

It is difficult for some singling pilgrims to learn how to identify, let alone befriend and express, anger. Or how to distinguish appropriate, reality-based anger from inappropriate anger—for example, anger that is a smoke screen to cover guilt. If you are having trouble sorting out your angry feelings, or if you are one of the multitude of those of us who were brought up to believe anger is wrong, once again: seek help.

7. Recovery. There comes a time (believe it!) when one's grieving days are done. The grieving has become history.

Some authorities call this "final stage" of grief "adaptation," and that's a good word. Singling by death does involve adapting to life after the death, or "life after Paul," as Arlene's minister put it. Fortunately, we humans are highly flexible beings. We have a marvelous capacity to adapt. Children adapt more easily than adults, to be sure, but all of us have seen adults too transcend tremendous losses—loss of a business, loss of a limb, loss of eyesight, loss of a child, loss of a spouse.

The term "recovery" is better than adaptation because it implies more. First, life is never static but is ever dynamic, always requiring adjustment to new circumstances. Our very future lies in our ability to recover from losses and keep on walking the singling path. Second, recovery hints at a principle many singles have proven: One can not only adapt to a significant loss; one can literally triumph and grow as a result.

Especially for the singling-by-death reader, we will share one more thought before we move on. While widows and widowers readily acknowledge the deaths of their spouses, when it comes to beginning the feeling, thinking, and behavior I call "singling" many of them drag their heels.

They resist singling more than divorced persons, for example. Maybe this is because they see their loss as greater, deeper, or more socially admirable. Maybe it is because they see themselves as "old" (even if the actuarial tables say they have one third or even a full half of their life still ahead of them). Whatever the reason, these folk have real difficulty, momentous difficulty, letting go of the past and embarking on their singling journey.

If this is you, please do read on. Widows and widowers who find it difficult to board the "single ship" can garner useful ideas from singles who come aboard at other ports.

4

Singling Because of Divorce

This book does not argue for divorce or against it. Its aim is to promote singling after divorce occurs: that is, to urge divorced persons to try singling before remarrying. There is a sound rationale for religious and cultural injunctions pertaining to divorce: namely, to affirm the ideal of faithfulness to commitments and to challenge people not to be capricious in giving up on relationships. Some people seek divorce when they might better achieve growth by remaining in their marriages and working on them. Others stay married, at least in the legal sense, when their relationship is irretrievably defunct and destructive. Loren, whose story follows, found out about his marriage as a consequence of his divorce.

> I never thought it could happen to me. For a fact, I didn't give divorce a thought at all.
>
> Now I know I should have. Now that it's all over, me a divorced man in California and Sheila and the kids back in Kentucky.
>
> I've been in therapy for a couple of months now. I went after the fact, skeptical as all get out but figuring "What the hell, my insurance will pay for it and I've gotta do something to get my head and my body back together," because my body was at the office but my head was someplace else most of the time. I've gotten more out of it than I expected.

When I started in therapy it was to prove what I already "knew"—that good old Loren was an OK guy while Sheila was a flaky dingbat throwing away fifteen years just when we were beginning to have it made.

. . . Throwing it all away because she just had to have the adolescence she says I stole from her when I married her while she was still a teenager. . . . Throwing it all away because she just had to find out what it would be like to date other men. Wow, how I wish I'd never told her I had sex in high school and college! I got so tired of her throwing it back at me: "You had your flings. You sowed your wild oats. You got it out of your system. It's my turn now," she'd say.

What I learned in therapy is that it takes two to make a relationship fly and two to shoot it down. I learned about what my therapist calls my "complicity in the demise of the marriage." I learned that when I decided California was the land of opportunity for me as an engineer and took a job out here, I should have asked Sheila what she thought. And when we got here, I should have paid attention to her, not just put every ounce of energy I had into my job to prove my decision was the right one.

I'm not just putting myself down. I tried to be a good father—if you can call a few hours a week with your kids being a good father. And I tried to be a good provider . . . no, I was a good provider. Of material things.

The hardest question my therapist asked was, "What are some of the things you did to drive her to leave you?" "Who, me?" I said, like "How could you imagine such a thing of Mr. Nice Guy?" But I've thought about it plenty since.

If I had known what I know now, I think we would still be together, or at least we *could* still be together. (*Long pause*) Well, OK, here's the hardest part, the thing I hate most to admit. If I'd known then what I know now I wouldn't have married Sheila in the first place. I don't know who or what I want in a wife, but whoever or whatever it is, it isn't Sheila. I guess she sensed that.

I don't even know whether I ever want to get married again. Maybe I'm just not cut out to be a husband and father. But then that *is* putting myself down, and my therapist says putting myself down won't help a thing.

Maybe it would be better to say that right now I don't know what I want out of life, period.

If Loren is still finding himself, surely most of us, like Yolanda, whose story follows, decide to do what we deem necessary for our preservation as persons.

From the moment I finally decided to leave Jerry, I felt relieved. I was so tired of waffling back and forth, back and forth. I'd long since had it with his mercurial temper . . . his possessiveness . . . his insistence on absolute control of all the money . . . his jealousy of my career and my friends . . . his refusal to go to counseling with me. I've been happier these five months without him than during my entire five years with him.

On the other hand, I'm very ambivalent about being a single career woman. In the five months since I got my own apartment I haven't had one date. That was just fine at first. I love my work and I have lots of fun with my friends. But I'll admit it's getting to me now. Loneliness is a problem. I don't want Jerry back. But it would be nice to have someone special who'd be number one to me and I could be number one to him.

Then there's my mother. She's a big help—what I mean is, with friends like her, who needs enemies? From the moment she found out Jerry and I were having trouble she said, "You made your bed; quit complaining and sleep in it." She thinks happiness has nothing to do with marriage! She thinks Jerry would have come around if I had just been patient. She still thinks I should go back to him.

(Pause. INTERVIEWER: What do you think?)

I think five years of patiently doing every little thing his way has just got to be enough! I'd rather be alone than with Jerry.

The Data of Divorce

Today one of every six adult Americans is, or has been, divorced. Currently, for every one hundred marriages contracted in the United States there are fifty divorces. The experts predict fewer first marriages in the 1990s, but more remarriages, accounting for a third of total marriages. Divorces, which escalated in the '70s but then dropped in 1982–83, are now heading up again. Some experts think at least half of baby-boom marriages will end in divorce.

Not long ago, couples who married young were the most vulnerable to divorce, and childless couples were the next most vulnerable. That is changing. We now witness a growing number of long marriages ending in divorce. (The highest increase in divorce today is among long-duration marriages.) Marriages with school-age children are also more susceptible than ever; for example, during 1988 there were over one million divorces in the United States with over one million children involved.

"Why?" many of us ask, as if knowing could solve the problem. Of course it cannot, but for the curious let me suggest that probably there are three main causes for today's divorces.

First, *there are fewer practical reasons for staying married than there used to be.* There are fewer children per marriage; there are slacker attitudes about parenthood; the roles of women are in rapid flux; there is more freedom regarding sexual matters; and our culture is generally accepting divorce as a part of life.

Second, *there are more idealistic and far vaguer expectations of marriage than our ancestors had.* In the early twentieth century, a young woman who sought to marry might have said, "I want a man to support me and give me children." Whether or not this expectation was met could be readily observed and measured within a few years, once she married. The bride either had a child, a roof over her head, and food on the family table, or she did not.

Today, a woman may seek marriage, saying, "I want to have someone to share things with." That is certainly a fine idea. But what is "sharing"? What is enough sharing? And when has a person satisfied the need to share? The goal is at best ambiguous, and each person's ideas of sharing and communication are individualistic and constantly changing. If the would-be sharer is emotionally non-single, the riddle is compounded, because a non-single person's need to share and be shared with may border on insatiable.

Third, *commitment has been replaced by contingency in our lifestyles.* Taking the marriage vows seriously is still the norm. But "till death do us part" has given way to "for as long as both of us choose to have this marriage." Divorce may not be viewed as a live option by newlyweds, but neither is it seen as out of the question.

There are pros and cons to this tendency of moderns to see the provisional, contingent nature of contemporary life, but I will leave discussion of such weighty matters to theologians and ethicists. People today view little as permanent or irrevocable; and the present situation is that singling by divorce is commonly chosen by a great many people. An equal number have divorce thrust upon them whether they want it or not. In the case of Loren at the beginning of this chapter, he is not quite accurate in suggesting that "it takes two to make a relationship fly and two to shoot it down." I have seen one partner "shoot it down" very effectively.

The Dynamics of Divorce

Divorcing is usually a very difficult process, even at its superficial edges. Note the following conversation, which took place during the coffee hour in the courtyard of a church:

LISA: Well, this will be my last Sunday in church for a while.
ANNE: What do you mean?
LISA: I don't think I'll be coming anymore.
ANNE: Why? (*Pause*) Lisa, what's wrong?
LISA: What's wrong is Tony and me. I've filed for divorce.
ANNE: Oh, I'm so sorry.
LISA: Don't be sorry. My marriage has been dead for a long time. I'm just finally getting around to burying it.
ANNE: Oh. Well, OK. I still am sorry, I must admit. But what does this have to do with church?

LISA: It's obvious, isn't it? Tony's family is here, not mine—and you know how Pastor Johnson feels about divorce! I'd be too embarrassed to show my face, especially since I'm the one who wants out. Don't worry. I've thought about this for a long time and I'll be OK. I just wanted you to know before you heard it from somebody else, since you and Jim have been friends.

ANNE: I still am your friend, Lisa.

LISA: Thanks. I needed that.

What do Lisa, Loren, Yolanda, and all singling-by-divorce persons have in common? As they begin singling, what growth tasks do they typically face? All divorced people are not the same, but are there some customary dynamics among them to which we ought to be sensitive? I believe there are.

Usually it makes little difference whether a singling adult happens to be the "divorcer" or the "divorced." By the "divorced" I mean the person involuntarily divorced at a spouse's insistence. In most cases it is painfully difficult either to be left by one's spouse or to leave one's spouse. There are variables from case to case, of course, such as those that follow when a person has been rejected in favor of a new lover or when children are in the picture. The pain of the rejecter may be of a different kind from the pain of the rejected one. But divorce always results in pain for both parties, and the pain can be enormous and all-consuming.

Pain. First, divorced people are people in pain. Not just newly divorced people either; I've seen divorced people in pain years after the fact. Whether it shows or not, whether they are even consciously aware of it or not, divorced people hurt. In their hurt, they long for somebody to say, "I accept you exactly as you are, with all that has happened in your life." At least it would be nice to have somebody convey the idea: "I want to be with you, to feel with you, and to try to understand." In short, the felt need is for someone to listen and care.

Our culture has no lack of advice givers; almost any neighbor, shopkeeper, or bartender will gladly offer advice. What is lacking is genuine care-giving. A caregiver is not necessarily a talker at all. It is someone who shows acceptance of the singling-by-divorce person, tolerance for what is happening, and readiness to be there to help the hurting person live through the pain until its growth potential is realized.

To care is to extend oneself, to offer oneself without prejudice or preachments. If you have a friend or two who are caregivers, you are indeed fortunate. Let them know you treasure them. Let them help. And if no one quite fits the bill, shop for and "hire" one—a skilled clergyperson, therapist, or other professional caregiver.

Anger. Second, divorced people are angry people. I have yet to meet a divorcing or recently divorced single who is not an angry person. If we define divorce-related anger as the reactive emotional response of a person to felt rejection, this is readily understood.

Rejection, or perceived rejection, accompanies divorce as a wake follows the path of a ship. Rejecters reject because they feel or fear rejection. Rejectees reject because they feel a need to protect themselves against the possibility of further rejection. Rejection itself tends to breed further rejection, and more anger.

However one gets it, the indispensable quality one needs is an it-is-all-right-to-be-angry attitude. The following exchange occurred in a support group for divorced persons:

SUSAN: I feel a lot of anger, but I shouldn't be angry. Tom and I had a lot of good years together. Even though I feel as if I just had to divorce him, I want it to be, you know, a friendly divorce.

CAROL: I thought like that too, for months and months. But now I know better, now that a couple of years have gone by. I feel like saying to you: "Susan, don't even bother to dream the silly dream of a friendly divorce."

LEADER: It would probably make more sense if you dreamed that your ex got run over by a steamroller. Only if there was no intense relationship in the first place can a couple have a friendly divorce. In such a case one might question whether they really had a marriage. (*Pause*) Divorce is not peaceable or civilized or logical. Divorce is an ordeal—an unwanted, untimely, crazy death.

SUSAN: I'm beginning to see what you mean.

LEADER: What interests me, Susan, is how are you doing with your anger?

At this point, the leader was able to help the group talk about ways to deal with anger in a healthy manner. How to deal well with anger is discussed in chapter 7, "Anger and Singling."

Crisis. A third dynamic is that divorced people are people in crisis. For one thing, divorce itself often causes crises even in the healthiest of adults—those who ordinarily take life's emergencies in stride. In addition, the weeks, months, and even years of strain following a marital breakup may render singling divorced persons more prone to additional crises—perhaps brought on by financial overextension, career upheaval, or nutritional neglect—than they would be under less stressful circumstances.

A crisis may be defined as a person's internal reaction to an external event of an emotionally hazardous nature. The events that trigger crises are most apt to be interpersonal in nature, and a key word in understanding crisis dynamics is the word "loss." Note the clarity of this theme in the following exchange between therapist and client:

THERAPIST: So Jane and the children have moved to Kansas.

JONATHAN: Yes. Just as I feared they would. I'm completely lost without them.

THERAPIST: That helps me understand why you seem so low.

JONATHAN: Not just low—lost. I guess I'm just a loser.

THERAPIST: You've sustained a gigantic loss, but you are certainly not a loser.

JONATHAN: I feel like one. Everything I had is gone.

Does this sound familiar? Jonathan is experiencing crisis.[1]

The Chinese word for crisis consists of two characters. The first character means "danger" and the second "opportunity."

To use a crisis constructively in one's life, one must see both the danger and the opportunity that are present.

Crises happen in us rather than to us. A crisis is a person's inner reaction to an outer event—a threat of loss or an actual loss—which arouses anxiety, guilt, depression, anger, panic, or terror.

Such a threatened or actual loss might not feel so catastrophic except that it exposes an identity problem within the individual, an identity problem that might otherwise have remained hidden. Therefore the crisis, however painful, can be used to confront one's own identity dilemmas and so enhance self-awareness and personal growth.

Because of the pain provoked by the crisis, however, it is difficult for the sufferer to look clearly within. She or he wants to run away from reality, to retreat to some familiar place of safety. The sufferer wants to cling to comfortable old dreams and favorite behaviors without facing the new identity that needs to emerge through the crisis.

One's reaction to a significant loss, such as the grief reaction, must be understood as one's response not only to losing a beloved person or status, but also *to losing one's old identity and dreams.* Such grief, however painful, can then be tempered by the awareness that a new identity is being born out of the ashes of the old. However, if a crisis is to serve the desired purpose of growth, the sufferer must use it as an opportunity to shed a cocoon and learn to fly. If the sufferer turns crisis grief into resistance, the opportunity to move to the next station on that person's growth road is lost.

Each crisis tends to happen at a point where something old is holding on and something new wants to emerge. Often, when an old dream or lifestyle has reached the limits of its value, a crisis occurs to tell us we are ready to move on. Now we must move into the new, unknown (and perhaps scary) dimensions . . . or stagnate.

Sometimes what was once our security or even our delight has become like a heavy weight that we drag with us. Insensitive to our tremendous potential for new development and expansion, we keep settling for less and less until our strange friend, the crisis producer, kicks us suddenly awake.

Crisis, then, is a condition wherein all our normal habits and supports are stripped down to nothing. We feel isolated from important others. We are tossed back upon our own resources even though we may not know what those resources are or how to use them.

Maybe, just maybe, we have been wrongly related to others and now, in our solitude, must discover something within ourselves before we can return to our community with a new attitude. Or maybe we need to find a new community.

A crisis is rarely just an annoying or destructive mishap to be done with. Instead, it is wise to view it as a possible door opener, a time to look at and reevaluate oneself. To the degree that one can decipher the meaning of a crisis experience, one can go with its flow rather than oppose it. Usually, however, people make their crises into problems to be endured, ignored, gotten over, drugged, hypnotized away, or cut out. We tend to see a crisis as a strange invader come to rip us off, to cheat us out of our hard-earned rewards.

We should consider, rather, that we can make most of our crises into stepping-stones. So let's make friends with the stranger, inviting its message to help us make the transition to our next level of growth. In this view, a crisis gives us a chance to see those dependencies and become free from those addictions which limit our aliveness, love, and freedom. What we hold on to, holds on to us. Jesus said, "Whoever seeks to save his life will lose it; and whoever loses it will save it, and live" (Luke 17:33, NEB).

Life Is a Mystery to Be Lived

Drop that which you hold
Let go of that to which you cling
Yield that for which you grasp
Release that to which you are attached

That which you hold, you lose
That which you resist, remains
That to which you are attached, imprisons
That which you surrender, frees

Embrace whatever comes
Flow with whatever happens

Understand whatever arises
Learn from each crisis you meet

For life is a mystery to be lived
Rather than a problem to be solved
And God a living moment to be acknowledged
Rather than a treasure to be kept

We must not kid ourselves into thinking that it is primarily another person or an outer situation that is handicapping us. Rather, it is usually our own inner beliefs and attitudes about ourselves that trap us. Often a crisis occurs when the outer fails and we have not yet discovered the power of the inner.

In this sense, a crisis may be something we have unconsciously helped to create and which we now consciously have to decode if we are to detect our needed change of direction. Maybe if we could have listened before it would not have taken such a blow to awaken us. Such a crisis could be compared to a tire blowout. We are angry that our trip has been interrupted; only later do we discover that ahead of us in the darkness was a chasm.

The felt danger of a crisis is that we have lost the fulfillment of our dreams. The actual danger is that we may never discover who the dreamer really is—that we may never know our best self and realize that the time of greatest loss may also be the time of greatest gain.

We humans rarely reach the point of arranging for our own self-change, and so life gives us an occasional assist toward change, often in the form of a crisis. If we feel (or indeed are) cheated, helpless, and undone, we might try remembering that the upset of the crisis may be God moving toward us in disguise, for God wears many garbs.

In a Crisis, Let Us Remember . . .

We cannot lose reality, only our dreams
We cannot lose truth, only our falseness
We cannot lose love, only our possessiveness
We cannot lose our self, only our ego
We cannot lose God, only our images

Therefore, let us use the grief of losing our dreams
To awaken to the joy of discovering our reality

Grief. Fourth, divorced people are grieving people. Marital separation usually precedes divorce, but separation is not the same as divorce. Even when divorce becomes final in the legal sense, emotional divorce may have occurred only partially. Grieving may have only just begun.

The feelings one has preceding the dissolution of a relationship are merely anticipatory; they never match those attending the final blow. One must still grieve after the actual loss has occurred. The grieving process of the singling-by-divorce person is virtually identical to that of the singling-by-death person. (You may want to review the discussion in chapter 3 now to make sure you understand the dynamics of grief.)

As we recall from chapter 3, after losing a spouse through death the grief process usually takes from *three to five years.* Divorce-related grief is often more complicated than postdeath grief, because along with the loss of an all-important relationship there can be additional emotional hurdles to overcome.

Some singling-by-divorce persons feel a deep sense of personal failure, like the woman who kept repeating, "No one has ever been divorced in my family—not on my mother's side, not on my father's side. No one ever, as far back as we can trace our roots. Until me—I had to be the one to blow it."

Other divorced persons experience setbacks in their grief process because ex-spouses or children, who have their own agendas and needs, are less than cooperative. One man's adult son flatly refused to attend his father's wedding, saying, "I'll be damned if I'll put my stamp of approval on that gold digger's scheme to rip off my inheritance!" Even if the wedding may have been premature or inappropriate, I was deeply touched by the wounded father's tears as he told his story at a singles workshop.

Still others find their own pain heightened by persisting pain in their childhood families. Curt, a man whose wife left him to follow her professional career goals, was already in a state of acute grief when his mother phoned to tell him, "My total sympathy is with Gaby. Before she married you I told her you'd be no prize. I don't see how anybody could ever live with you." Curt had to be reminded that his mother had herself been divorced and was now separated from her new husband.

In these and other ways some singling-by-divorce persons feel as if they have every emotional "illness" one could catch. Often they become additionally distressed or depressed over feeling that way. Difficulties and cruelties like these can slow down or freeze the grief process, which is why caring friends, a therapist, and a support group are invaluable to the life of a divorced person trying to start singling.

Please understand this: Feeling heartsick, body-sick, or "crazy in the head" (or, as one counselee put it, "berserko") is common among the divorced, especially the newly divorced. Most divorced singles not only know that they are feeling bad; they have accurate ideas about what they feel and why, and they can articulate them. They will say they feel alone, lost, or grief-stricken, and they will tell you why: "I don't know if I'll ever see my daughter again."

One reason singling by divorce typically begins from such a painful starting place is that the marriage has usually been a disappointing experience. The expectations most people bring to marriage are to some degree exaggerated and unrealistic.

But divorce is an even more disappointing experience than marriage, and disappointment is a much underrated emotion. It hurts, it embarrasses, it gnaws and jabs and harasses, it upsets one's sense of balance and purpose. The sense of loss that comes with divorce is just plain awful. It really is all right to grieve. As one single put it, "I grieved like hell for the three longest years of my life." The man who made that statement was one of the healthier singles of my acquaintance. He was ministering to others by leading a "divorce recovery group" sponsored by his synagogue.

Dependency. Fifth, divorced people are dependent people. To be human is, of course, to be dependent. It is the trait within all of us that insists upon confirmation of our worth by others. In itself, this need is natural and healthy. However, normal dependency often becomes greatly intensified under the stress of divorce. One counselee, during her postdivorce adjustment period, wrote:

> I've always known I was needful, but now I feel superneedful. I've been a mite off-balance before, but now I'm mightily imbalanced. I used to get pangs of skin hunger occasionally, but these days my whole body longingly cries to be held. My self-esteem periodically got shaky, but now it has fallen flat on its face. Worst of all, my confidence in my ability to select appropriate people as soul friends was at an all-time high when I trusted myself to Jack to be his wife "till death do us part." But right now I wouldn't trust myself to pick an edible piece of fruit out of a whole orchard full of ripe peaches.

Because I knew the writer well and she was now far away, I answered her letter in part as follows:

> I think it is good, Joan, that you are so in touch with your dependency needs. You seem wiser and in a good position to learn more about all of your inner dynamics—to understand them, own them, respect their power, flow with them, and even embrace them. If you can do that, I think there will come some joy one day—maybe even pretty soon. To help, I'd suggest you seek a support group of women with whom you can share your journey. Why not seek out such a group in the church you attend? And if there isn't such a group already formed, why not start one?

Within a few months, I received another letter from Joan. She had found a support group; her time of pain, anger, crisis, grieving, and "superdependency" had largely passed. She had come to a place of relative calm, an oasis of peace along her singling way.

5

Singling Because of Delay

Having addressed the needs of people who are singling because their marriages ended, we now turn to those singling by delay. For some people, singling by delay is preferable to singling by divorce (let alone death), even if the delay is very long. They want to be married, but they want to do it right. They are choosy.

Others believe they have no choice in the matter. They want to be married too, but even if it takes forever they must wait for their marital ship to come in bearing Mr. or Ms. Right. And when it does: "Somehow I'll just know." Here is Lucille's story.

> I cannot remember a time when I didn't like boys. It isn't exactly that I didn't like girls; but I always liked boys more. My earliest memory is playing with the boys in my neighborhood and feeling superior because they wanted me.
>
> I also cannot remember a time when I didn't want to get married. When I was seven I had already picked a husband, a boy named P.J. As it turns out, my intuition was terrific; P.J. is one of the most desirable men I know—handsome, wealthy, powerful, and still a really nice guy. Trouble is, of course, he married somebody else.
>
> That's the story of my life: always the bridesmaid, never the bride. I don't know another thirty-five-year-old, male or female, who's been in more weddings than me. I'll bet I've "stood up" for twenty friends at least. I've even stood up

for my former boyfriends. Really, have you ever heard of a "best woman"? Well, that's me—I've been the "best woman" at a wedding and I've got the photos to prove it. The groom was an only child, and when he explained to his fiancée that I was his oldest friend, like the sister he always wanted but never had, she understood perfectly. In fact, she asked my advice about how to make her marriage work!

I also cannot remember a time when I didn't want to be a mother. At almost thirty-six, with the time clock running, that's getting a bit scary, you know?

I'm almost six feet tall, and I know I'm no raving beauty. But I'm neat, clean, healthy, good-looking, well-dressed, hardworking, smart, honest, and successful in my career. I've never been one to chase after men, but all the men I know know I like men and they sure know I'm available. I'm a member of several clubs; I get invited to parties; I'm active in my church and community; yet I can hardly remember the last time I was on a real live date with a real live man. It's damn discouraging, to say the least.

(Later in the interview) What I want to know is, What's the matter with me? Where did I go wrong? Am I not aggressive enough? Why can't I live a normal life like everybody else?

Lucille's questions merited an immediate response. What I tried to convey is: Nothing is the matter with you, Lucille. From what we know about you, you did not "go wrong." You can live a normal life—being unmarried is not abnormal. And by the way, what makes you think "everybody else" is living a normal life?

One might assume that Lucille's husband-to-be is simply late in arriving, like a delayed airplane, meaning that her fulfillment has (alas) just been deferred for a time. But the term "delay" is too limited. Lucille might have told quite a different tale at twenty-six, but at thirty-six she is not only feeling single by delay, she is also feeling single by default and, not having made peace with singlehood as a way of life, she remains wistfully non-single in her heart. So hers is more than an inconvenience.

It has become a serious situation, and she is asking, "Where did I go wrong?"

What if this husband-to-be is never to be? Will Lucille ever fulfill her longing to be a mother? I hope so, but better to do it as a single parent (by adopting a child, for example) than by settling for whomever she can get to marry her!

Single by Default

When I say that Lucille's singleness was not only by delay but also by default, what do I mean by default?

Other terms might seem benign by comparison—deferment, postponement, inertia, or plain delay. The world of the never married and formerly married, however, is populated with many like Lucille who in their own estimation (or imagination) are single by "default," in the simple dictionary meanings of that word: a failure or neglect to do something one is supposed to do; or an absence from something (as a legal proceeding or a competition) where one should appear. The observant reader probably noticed I did not say *"singling* by default." Perhaps I should have said "non-single by default," for these people are single only in the technical sense. They are the great number of people, whether never married or formerly married, who view marriage as normative, or even as the only decent way to live. They are waiting for fate, or God, or the stars, to present to them their destined mate. They view their single estate as a static condition, an unavoidable prelude, interlude, or postlude to "normal" or "real" living. Real living is The Concert, and all seats at The Concert are reserved for twosomes.

So they think of themselves as persons who have been overlooked, have failed to show up in the right place at the right time, are just unlucky, or are doomed to an unmercifully long wait for their ship to come in so that their singleness can end. Some become cynical and bitter through the years. A never-married man said, "All the women are after is money and good looks. I'll be damned if I'll go out and buy a BMW and dress for success just to score with some bimbo who couldn't spot a man of substance if she tripped over him." Others are more philosophical: If it's to be, it will be.

But whatever their reaction, the years pass and *they do not put energy into singling because they do not believe in the legitimacy of singlehood.*

A never-married man in his late twenties asked his minister: "If marriage is ordained by God, why have I been kept waiting so long?" The minister replied: "Marriage may be God's will for some, but not for everybody. Could be you aren't ready for it. Or maybe you've expected God to drop a mate into your lap without doing your part. Or perhaps being married isn't the best way for you to live." The young adult, who did not like his pastor's response, was single by default.

I do not mean to judge this group of "non-single singles" harshly. Actually, I admire them. To become coupled at any level, a person has to either make something happen, or perhaps follow the path of least resistance and permit someone else to make something happen on their behalf. Thus, I heartily congratulate the Lucilles of this world for being noncompliant and nonconformist. Resistance, even recalcitrance, evidences strength. This is a group of potentially powerful singles.

If you fit into this group, congratulations for the gift of discrimination. Generally anybody can find a mate if any mate will do. But a "nice woman" and a "nice man" do not necessarily make a nice couple. We all see tragic examples. For many years I knew a married couple who hated each other, put each other down mercilessly, and essentially lived alone together in separate bedrooms of the same house. Believe it or not, each was a warm, intelligent person when the other one was not present! More recently I met a sensitive, talented woman who lived with (and seemed clearly mated to) a retarded, multiply handicapped cousin many years her senior. There were extenuating circumstances, to be sure; but there were numerous other options too, and hers was a very confining life.

In contrast, it is considered perfectly normal in Western, civilized cultures for a person to wait and wait "until the right one comes along" and then, only then, to couple up. Few people would dispute the untold suffering connected with marrying too soon or marrying the wrong person. Almost everyone would agree that it is better not to marry at all than to endure the pain of so grave an error in timing or judgment . . . almost everyone, that is, except certain people who find themselves interminably and annoyingly noncoupled by the fateful circumstance of "default." But let us now turn to a more gentle word: delay.

Single by Delay

What do I mean by delay?

In a culture where coupling is considered everyone's right and right for everyone, most people put off, as long as they can, coming to a conscious awareness that they need to make a decision about singling. They keep their hope alive, the hope that their lives can be "normal"—meaning lived within a primary relationship—not realizing that coupling is not normal for everybody at every stage of life. Nor do they realize that singlehood doesn't just happen (remember, it's much more than a condition of the law). One has to make it happen, and that requires a decision and a design.

I remember when I was a child in an immigrant neighborhood in Detroit asking my mother and grandmother about certain folk in our community who were obviously grown up but unmarried. Some of them were widows or widowers. This was considered "too bad," especially if they were women whose husbands had been killed in the war or women who were now too old or too poor or too unattractive ever to remarry.

Others, I was told, had simply never married at all. They had "waited too long," or "Mr. Right never came along," or "She couldn't find anyone who wanted to marry her," or even "Her trouble is she was always too fussy." These were the pat answers if my question was about a woman. If my question was about a man, the responses were apt to be even more stereotyped. Any never-married adult male was "an old bachelor," "too set in his ways," peculiar beyond belief, and probably the victim of habits so strange as to be unmentionable. In any case, I was to steer clear of him!

The absolute assumption a generation ago seemed to be that no sane adult ever *chose* not to marry. Religious celibacy might have been the exception, but even priests and nuns and nonmarried missionaries were thought to have given up the holy calling of matrimony only for the sake of an even holier calling, to serve God and humankind. In the church I attended as a youth, when women were not yet being ordained, it was publicly stated that the only reason so many single women were overseas missionaries was that the men destined to be their husbands had refused to hear or heed the call of God.

Now, forty years later, living as we do in an age of high technology and liberation if not license, one would think the situation must be vastly different. Surely there has been some change, has there not? At least most of us try to avoid stereotyping and labeling people nowadays—except when describing singles! Even today few people in this supposedly enlightened age talk or act as if singling is worthwhile, or as if singlehood is anything but a forerunner of marriage or of living together. Again and again, the single life gets pegged as a less-than-normal condition characterized not in terms of what it is or has to offer but in terms of what it supposedly lacks. People assume a significant absence.

Society today includes just as many adults who are single, at least statistically, as there are married couples; that is, one of every three adults is nonmarried.[1] Most of us are aware of our perennially high divorce rates and countless unhappy marriages. Still, the unspoken, unwritten assumption for most of us, old and young, straight and gay, married and nonmarried, seems to be that singleness surely must be a temporary condition. It is a condition of making do until the right person comes along and the better way can be realized. People persist in claiming and insist on telling themselves that the real way to live is, of course, in a relationship. Not in relationships, mind you; in a relationship with a "one and only." No wonder these folks don't decide to start singling. Who wants to learn how to live with a "cancer" when the cure surely lies just around the corner?

As a consequence, many good people remain "non-single singles"—single (in a way) by default or delay, but refusing to begin singling in earnest because they prefer to believe the fairy-tale themes immortalized by a multitude of our "national anthems" such as "Some Enchanted Evening," "Some Day My Prince Will Come," and "Someone to Watch Over Me."

If these and other songs symbolize your kind of fable, you can choose to continue to live in its thrall. Or you may want to accompany me as I look at singling by design.

6

Singling by Design

The path to singlehood is no freeway. It is more like a mine field. There are trail markings, way stations, and clues as to where the "mines" might be. A travel plan is a good idea, however. It is also important to really want to make the trip, because the trip isn't just fun and games.

The Biggest Fear

I have asked hundreds of newly singling people, most of them in midlife (mid-thirties to mid-fifties), what scares them most about the journey. I expected that it would be fear of being alone or of the unknown, and those are common singling fears. But the most common response goes something like this:

> I'm afraid that the more single I become the less I will want to be with others. I'm afraid I will get too set in my single ways, just as I have been too set in my non-single ways. I will get so locked in to singlehood that I won't recognize Ms. or Mr. Right before my very eyes. I'm afraid of becoming too independent, self-contained—even a recluse. It is already difficult for me to reach out to others now, and I'm afraid it will get harder yet.

You may recall our continuum from chapter 1:

Non-Single		Slightly Single		Somewhat Single			Mostly Single		Wholly Single	
0	1	2	3	4	5	6	7	8	9	10

Let's assume, for a moment, that as you progress on the path toward singlehood, your inventory of singling tools gradually grows complete. Whereas you began a "0" at birth and felt like no more than a "2" the day your mate left, lo and behold! It is now five years later and you have singled so wonderfully well you have become a "9" (nobody's perfect).

Meanwhile, what has become of your non-single skills? Have they evaporated? eroded? gotten dull and rusty?

Have no fear, singling pilgrim. Some people begin life with a bent toward autonomy—the strong-willed child, for example—and a rare few may be born loners. But most of us begin as highly affiliative, dependent folk, naturally good at non-single behaviors; and *if your non-single skills were a 9 then, they remain a 9 now,* the same semiperfect level your singling skills have become after years of concentrated practice. Some of your non-singling skills may include basic trust in the goodness of life and the ability to connect with others, to give and receive care, and to show your feelings. Now you can look forward to living your life with a highly developed set of singling skills *and* a highly developed set of non-single skills!

You see, the good news is that the single life can be an exciting concert rather than merely a prelude, interlude, or postlude. The bad news is that no one is born with singling skills. Like the skills of a concert artist, singling skills must be acquired. We Americans want shortcuts, as did the busy businesswoman who opined, tongue-in-cheek, how nice it would be if she could produce a baby in one month because that's all the time she felt she could afford. But there are no shortcuts. One can learn how to conduct the single life, but it takes intelligent practice, and intelligent practice takes time.

Singling skills are "add-ons." They are skills we must acquire by decision and design if we are to have them at all. Non-single skills, whatever yours may be for good or for ill, come naturally.

You already had them when you cried mercilessly for your midnight feeding, whether your mother got any sleep or not. By the time you were a toddler you had the non-single life down to a science, and during your preteens you developed it into an art. If you are a parent, you know this, because you see it in your children.

As stated in chapter 1, what happens to one's non-single skills on the way to singlehood is that they become more cultured and refined, less crude or crass. It is analogous to learning a second language: The grammar, syntax, vocabulary, and literacy often improve in the learner's original language. But it is because one's early habit patterns (non-single skills) never leave that it is quite impossible to become too single for one's own good. To put it another way, the trick is to become as single as you can—just as single as you are non-single already. Once you have done that, you will be able to keep your single and non-single sides in creative tension with each other.

Fear of the Unknown

Newly divorced after thirty years of marriage, Lydia admitted her fear. "At forty-eight, I know I may be only half through with my life," she said, "but I feel nothing but dread. I don't know who I am anymore, or who's 'out there,' or what I'm supposed to be doing to 'get with it,' or what in the world 'it' is I'm supposed to get with. I just feel lost."

Lydia was born in 1939. If you were born in the 1930s, '40s, or '50s, you were probably reared with presuppositions about God, country, marriage, and the family. You assumed, for instance, that if you treated other people justly you would be dealt with in a fair way too. Many of us "knew" God was on our side (or at least neutral), and if we paid due respect, we could count on God's providential care, constancy, and protection. When our teachers talked about the American way of life, they spoke as if they knew what it was. We thought we knew too. And we thought we knew what marriage was, and what the family was. It all seemed sure.

By contrast, as we approach the twenty-first century it all seems very unsure—fluid, contingent, slippery, up for grabs.

Social and behavioral scientists and even theologians hardly know how to talk about these things today, except to say we are now a pluralistic, multiethnic, multicultural society with a great variety of identities and lifestyle options. This may be off-putting to folk who like things simple and clear, but it is certainly not bad. Singlehood, for instance, is now a live option as never before in human history, however scary it feels to a non-single person singling reluctantly.

But some of us stubbornly resist change. We'd rather not "go with the flow." No, thank you. We need, indeed we demand, security and continuity. Are these not our inalienable rights? They are not.

Security and continuity cannot be found in what America was or who we were in the middle of the twentieth century. The world isn't that kind of place anymore, if it ever was. The world does not owe us a living. In fact, no one "owes" us anything. Living in today's world is an insecure existence for everybody. There are no exceptions unless perhaps the very rich, but even the U.S. dollar, the Swiss franc, and the Japanese yen are subject to rapid change nowadays. It is an insecure world.

In our insecurity, then, the onset of singleness brings with it an identity crisis, and, as Charles Gerkin observed,

> coping with crisis . . . requires the capacity to transcend the past, move through the change of the present, and *embrace the open-ended, unknown quality of the future.*[1]
>
> Persons undergoing the necessity of life's transformations must find their way into the transformed life on the terms of *their own* response. . . . The new reality will become real for them only as it becomes an ingredient within *their own* way of symbolizing and interpreting their experience.[2]

Difficult though it may be, you must risk making your own personal journey on the path to singlehood. Until you take that risk, what this sage calls "the new reality" cannot be yours.

Good News

The good news is: You do not have to travel alone. You can take your faith (be it ever so small), your spiritual guide, your therapist, a few choice books, and a personal friend or two or even three or more. This is the time to take inventory of these resources and use them. If you don't have them now, find them, shop for them! Many churches and synagogues, for example, have excellent programs and organizations explicitly designed to provide such resources for single adults. Other specific suggestions will be found in the following chapters and the annotated bibliography. Note especially chapters 9, "Friendship and Singling," and 11, "Where to Find Help."

Reading this book and following through on its ideas will help, but still it may all feel strange and scary. Perhaps you can take some small comfort in reminding yourself that you are not the first pilgrim on a trip into the unknown. Years ago, one such traveler composed a prayer that has helped many:

> Lead, kindly Light, amid the encircling gloom,
> Lead Thou me on!
> The night is dark, and I am far from home—
> Lead Thou me on.
> Keep Thou my feet; I do not ask to see
> The distant scene—one step enough for me.[3]

Your Two Selves

Each of us has been endowed with both a "safekeeping self" and an "experimental self."[4] They can be described in chart form.

The Safekeeping Self	*The Experimental Self*
Is serious and cautious	Is fun-loving and impetuous
Avoids risks	Takes risks
Thinks, analyzes, evaluates	Feels, guesses, uses seeming irrelevance to grasp meaning
Is careful not to wish too much	Makes impossible wishes
Punishes mistakes, is intolerant of deviations from perfection	Learns by trial and error, accepts imperfection as part of life
Makes rules	Breaks rules

Comforts, reassures, soothes pain	Challenges, invites some pain
Is suspicious and skeptical	Is trustful and curious
Is alert to danger, with an eye on the consequences	Is open to anything
Avoids surprises	Likes surprises
Concerned with here-and-now experience, in touch with conscious reality	In touch with the unconscious, can "touch" total experience
Never plays till work is done	Delays work till play is done
Avoids errors	Doesn't mind being wrong
Is logical and fact-oriented	Imagines, intuits, speculates
Abhors confusion	Does not mind being confused
Wants it finished, wraps it up	Learns how to keep doing it
Guides and supports	Recognizes patterns, makes connections
Avoids interstate highways, avoids speeding	Makes life-and-death decisions while driving down an interstate highway at 5 mph over the speed limit

Both selves are useful. One would not want to walk through life with only the safekeeping self. Neither would one want to make the journey with only the experimental self. Balance is important. Clearly, however, it is the safekeeping self that fears the unknown. If fear of the unknown is your fear, now is the ideal time to invite the experimental self into your life in a heightened way. It is appropriate to have the experimental self in the pilot's seat on your singling trip. It is just as appropriate to have the safekeeping self firmly ensconced in the copilot's seat. With both selves working as a team, you will not crash.

Fear of Being Alone

Deciding to become single can leave one feeling very much alone. Having the decision made for you can leave you feeling even more alone, which is one reason why choosing singlehood is probably easier than having it choose you. Either way, for some people the very thought of singlehood evokes great fear of aloneness. If you want to become truly single, it is important that you keep this fear from paralyzing you.

Loneliness is OK; lonesomeness isn't. Let us examine and redefine some terms to distinguish the positive aspects of aloneness from its negative possibilities.

If we look for a dictionary definition, a main meaning of single is "lone," and the term "single" may be offered as a primary synonym for the word "alone." Thus, singleness and aloneness can be synonymous.

"Aloneness," however, means not only separate, apart or isolated from others, but also unique, unequaled, or even unexcelled, as in the sentence "She is alone among her peers in devotion to her career." "Loneliness" is virtually identical to aloneness, although in a heightened sense loneliness may also connote "without company or companionless."

To put it another way, aloneness simply is a state of being, neither good nor bad, and loneliness is the feeling dimension of aloneness.

There is no denying loneliness. Loneliness is inescapably interwoven into the fabric of one's aloneness. Remember: A person will experience aloneness and loneliness whether single or not. To live and love is to be alone and feel lonely.

One who is skilled at singling as well as at non-singleness will be more able to use solitude creatively than one who is not. It is entirely possible for a person to be creatively lonely; that is, aloneness and loneliness can be positive and useful. They can enhance one's singling skills.

Aloneness and loneliness are most clearly seen in sharp contrast to "lonesomeness," which cannot be positive. Lonesomeness plainly points to a depressed state of being alone—a sad or disquieting feeling of isolation. It conveys a longing for companionship, as in the old song "Oh, Lonesome Me!"

Loneliness can be all right, then—not fun, and not necessarily desirable, but certainly tolerable. Lonesomeness, on the other hand, is always problematic. The following chart may help you clarify the difference between "lonely" and "lonesome":

Where LONELIness is to feel unloved,
LONESOMEness is to feel unlovable.

Where LONELIness is to feel distance from a friend,
LONESOMEness is to feel there is no friend regardless of distance.
Where LONELIness is to have been hurt in loving,
LONESOMEness is to hurt because I am unwilling to risk loving.
Where LONELIness is a friend challenging a value I hold dear,
LONESOMEness is having no friend who cares enough to challenge any of my values.
Where LONELIness is chancing to meet someone I was once close to,
LONESOMEness is never to have risked being close to anyone.
Where LONELIness is to have made an enemy,
LONESOMEness is never to have offended anybody.
Where LONELIness is being on the outs with someone I love,
LONESOMEness is avoiding conflict with someone I love for fear of losing that person.
Where LONELIness is a shattered dream,
LONESOMEness is removing myself from the possibility of dreaming.
Where LONELIness is reaching out and having my overture ignored or rebuffed,
LONESOMEness is being unwilling to reach out anymore.[5]

Learning Friend-Making

This story is about me.

"When are you going to go after the friends you want in your life, instead of just processing whoever happens to show up?"

It was almost ten o'clock, near the end of our session, when Harold—my therapist—asked the question. I stared at him with a dull heart and blank mind.

It had been just weeks since my estranged wife, our son, and the family dog had moved to the East Coast. I was working as a psychotherapist specializing in marriage and family therapy, my divorce was nearly final, and I had now become a "psychotherapy patient" for the first time since finishing my own training as a therapist. I had chosen Harold because he was reputed to be the best.

His question hit me hard. When are you going to go after the friends you want in your life? It haunted me all day long. When are you going to go after the friends you want in your life? It kept me awake most of the night. *When are you going to go after the friends you want?* As I brooded over the question I realized that in my entire life I had never intentionally, assertively made a friend—a friend *I* chose, one *I* wanted, not as a business associate, teacher, or romantic partner, but as a friend.

It wasn't that I had no friends. I had had friends from early childhood. But friendships happened or they didn't. I either let them happen or I didn't. Certainly I had never made one happen. I had wooed and won teachers, training opportunities, employers, and lovers; but never had I courted a friend for my life. I hadn't even thought about it.

On that sleepless night a main goal for my singling journey was born: "I want to learn how to make a friend."

That was more than a dozen years ago. My life has never been the same. How glad I am!

What about you? Initially I thought my lack was peculiar to me, perhaps a by-product of my being an only child. Or was it my maleness? But as I have shared my story, many other men and women have identified a similar pattern in their lives. They let their friends choose them too. Just as I did.

Still it is fair to say that women, even if quite non-single, are often more able friend makers than men. Male pride ("I'm a big boy, I can do life all by myself") gets in the way. My first attempt at courting a friend was amazingly difficult for me. Fortunately, the result was astonishingly rewarding.

One of my treasured female friends, considerably younger than I but very skilled at friend-making, points out that we live in a culture that teaches and rewards intentionality in two kinds of relationships—coupling/marriage, and parenting.[6] I think there may be a third, namely, career relationships—for instance, currying favor with the boss's family to win a promotion.

Society simply does not endorse friendship on the same plane. Try getting into a hospital's intensive care unit to see a dear friend to whom you are not "related." It's far easier if you are the patient's uncle from Carbuncle. Try requesting time off from work to be with a special friend in need. You may well risk having your boss think you immature, unhealthily dependent, or oriented to your same sex.

Chapter 9 deals with making friends, and chapter 12 has hints about living alone. Right now I want to underscore that your singling skills in both of these areas can be developed. Together they form an unbeatable antidote to your fear of being alone. The idea is to not just let life happen. The idea is to make life happen.

Develop Your Own Action Plan

Part Three of this book concerns practical matters. Its chapters discuss issues singling pilgrims have raised about how to travel, how to "get there"; policies they have found critical to their journeys; and procedures they have found helpful. To include every topic of concern to every singling adult would be impossible. I have, however, included those most requested by workshop participants and counselees alike.

The chapters approach each topic in terms of traps to avoid and goals to pursue—how to keep from undermining oneself, on the one hand, and how to steer one's ship toward the port of singlehood, on the other hand.

With this in mind, you may read the remaining chapters in any order; that is, read first the chapter that intrigues you most, then the one that interests you next, and so on. In so doing you are ordering your priorities and charting your own course. It is true, I placed the chapters in an order that makes sense to me. If your safekeeping self prefers to read the chapters in my order, that's all right; no one will know.

PART THREE

Pathways

7

Anger and Singling

The first major mine field along the singling path is anger. If one does not know how to defuse the mines of anger, they will blow up in one's face over and over again, and the would-be single will remain a non-single person. Listen to Steve's story.

> I spent the first twenty years of my life trying to win my parents' approval.
>
> My father—may he rest in turmoil—my father rarely noticed that I existed. When he did notice, it was because Mother insisted he administer punishment for my bad behavior. She insisted it was his job, and besides, she would say, she had no idea what had gotten into me this time but it must be my father's genes because it was beyond her ken and, anyway, punishing bad boys was a man's job, so why didn't he conduct himself like a real man for goodness' sake? . . .
>
> Honest to God, she really talked like that. She still does.
>
> I said my father only noticed the bad behaviors Mother called to his attention. Well, my mother was something else again. She noticed absolutely everything. I swear she paid attention to every waking moment of my day. She's still proud that she had me toilet-trained at eight months of age, which means she had herself trained to notice even the slightest reddening in her little darling's face. I could never be neat enough or clean enough, and nothing I could do was ever good enough. She loved to say things like,

> "God gave you so-o-o-o much. Why don't you live up to it for once?"
>
> After I finished high school I continued living at home and commuted to college because Mother insisted I was too young and immature for dormitory life. "After all," she said to my father when he suggested that I go away to college, "our Stevie's nothing but a spoiled only child who needs a mother to wait on him hand and foot." Of course Father just sat there, as always. "It's best to let her have her say and her way," he used to say.
>
> Well, after taking her crap for twenty years I finally got out. The only time I've ever gone back into that house was for my father's funeral and, frankly, that was once too often.

Steve went on to explain that at age twenty he and a woman he was dating eloped after they became pregnant. The marriage was rocky from the start, and although Steve tried to please his bride she left him immediately after their child was stillborn.

In the wake of his divorce he joined the Navy. He barely tolerated military life ("It was too much like home"), and when I met him he had received an honorable discharge and was back in college.

Steve struck me as very intelligent. I later learned he had been valedictorian of his high school class, and he always got A's in college. But Steve impressed me as a cold, empty old man of twenty-four—polite and verbally skilled but withdrawn, skeptical, and seething. Though not in touch with his rage, he was clearly angry at his parents, himself, and the world. His sullen disposition and volatile behavior had thwarted his chances for a tuition grant, and he had been advised to seek professional help for his emotional problems.

The Root of Anger

When all the efforts one puts into a task (or a relationship) are overlooked, when good intentions are ignored, or when all that is noted is one's failure to measure up to others' expectations, a person reflexively experiences a sense of injustice and rejection, as Steve did. The reaction is that of rage, whether the rage is expressed overtly or not.

Anger has already been discussed as one of the dynamics of grief in the context of singling by death (chapter 3). It was also discussed as a dynamic of divorce (chapter 4). So why devote a chapter to anger now?

There are several reasons. First, if you are an angry person like Steve, singling is sure to fan the flames of your anger because singling requires assertiveness. Steve was reared to be non-single and to swallow his anger, storing it inside. That is how he functioned in his childhood family, in his brief marriage, and in the Navy. Now Steve's approach to anger had outlived whatever value it once held for him. Now he needed to learn to operate differently, but even though he wanted to learn a better way, the very prospect angered him all the more. Steve's may be an extreme case, but a lot of non-single people are brought up to swallow their anger.

Second, anger actually comprises a whole "family" of emotions, and the singling person must surely wrestle with some of them. In the context of the kinds of people-dynamics with which singling is concerned, anger may be defined to include any emotional reaction of a person to rejection, real or imagined. Here is just a sampling of expressions manifesting anger:

"I am irritated with you."
"When I hear her voice on the other end of the telephone my stomach starts to churn."
"I resent that."
"I hate it when you use that tone of voice and get that look on your face."
"You hurt me bad."
"He walked out on us more than three years ago; you'd think I could quit feeling bitter about it."
"I never want to see that S.O.B. again as long as I live."
"I don't know what it is, but there's something about her that bugs the hell out of me. I can't stand to be around her."
"Knowing how he did his best to destroy me, I'd give anything to see him get what's coming to him."

Let us not forget "righteous indignation" and all sorts of rage or outrage, whether of mild or great intensity. All these are varieties of anger. Almost everybody experiences a few of them.

Third, the "anger family" of emotions is particularly apt to surface during a time of change. You may not be as angry as Steve, or in the same way, or for the same reasons. But if you are serious about singling, chances are you are nonetheless an angry person.

I am. I do 100 percent better with my anger now than during those awful years when I kept dealing knockdown blows to my marriage while insisting that I was trying to save it. Finally I achieved a knockout. I was like the politicians who insist we are fighting for peace, killing people only if absolutely necessary for their own sake, while saying, "Me, a hawk?" Anyway, I divorced in 1973 but my anger still comes, at the oddest times. Now I just deal with it more effectively than I used to. And when people act as if they do me a favor by graciously permitting me to minister in their midst although I am permanently tainted by divorce, anger still wells up within me.

Fourth, anger is an automatic, involuntary response. Anyone who feels left out, shut out, cut off, or deliberately pushed away from a desired relationship reacts automatically with anger. Under such circumstances, anger seems to have only one message, simple and graphic. As one singling woman, Hannah, put it in an imaginary conversation with her ex-husband, whom she saw as consistently writing her off:

> Damn it, I am a precious human being, and you refuse to see that fact! I hate the way you see me. I hate the way you keep treating me. I hate the way you keep trying to use me. I hate the way you go out of your way to put me down. It hurts so much that I demand you stop it. Stop it! *Stop it now!*

In one sense Hannah was giving her power away in her demand, by letting her ex "get to" her—allowing his attitudes and actions to determine how she felt. However, in another sense hers was a legitimate demand. Given Hannah's situation as co-owner of a business (which she founded) with her ex-husband, and co-parent with him, her anger was quite appropriate.

In fact, anger is the emotional lifeblood of a singling person like Hannah. It affirms the priceless nature of one's own essential being and settles for no less than the same affirmation from others. Hannah's case is memorable because she was a remarkably strong woman who had been divorced for some years and was quite single, while her ex-husband was a vacillating man who had unsuccessfully remarried and divorced twice. In general, Hannah was dealing with her life beautifully. Yet anger continued to plague her.

To be sure, anger can stem from other sources besides those mentioned here. For many of us, however, rejection-related anger seems an inevitable accompaniment to singling. I have known few singling persons who did not need to deal with it.

Dealing with It

What matters most is not the getting rid of anger once and for all; one may not be able to remove its source. What matters is learning how to deal with it as it comes.

Remember, singlehood means neither having to "attach" oneself to another person like a clinging vine nor having to "detach" from everybody to prove one's independence. Singlehood implies the freedom and power to operate interdependently as one chooses. In the process of singling, then, one's skill in handling anger plays an important role in determining whether one becomes wholly single or not, because how one handles anger can literally determine whether one enjoys satisfying interpersonal living or not. Non-singles may be able to keep people in their lives who, because they are also non-single, tolerate their sullen moods or temper tantrums, but singlers who want mature friends can ill afford such childish luxuries.

Non-single or single, the way anger is handled has great bearing on the lifestyles of all of us in our relationships with others. From the styles of those who tend in varying degrees to "bottle up" anger to the styles of those who tend in varying degrees to "spew out" anger, there is a continuum. At one end we find withdrawn, submissive, dependent, and even self-punishing individuals. At the other end are aggressive, domineering, and even punitive individuals.

Somewhere in the middle, between the extremes, are those persons who have learned to neither bottle up anger nor spew it out. Rather, they have come to recognize anger as the positive, self-affirming emotion it can be. They use its energy positively, both to correct their own inappropriate attitudes and actions and to confront antagonists with their need to do the same. They have learned what needs to be done to correct the cause of anger, and to do it each time anger comes, "cash and carry," while the emotions are fresh and new. They might not identify themselves as "single," but they are masters of at least one major singling skill—handling anger.

There are a number of useful models for handling anger creatively. But so powerful are one's habitual ways with anger and so crucial is the singling task of learning a better way that I strongly urge the serious singler to *(a)* do some reading on the topic;[1] *(b)* enroll in an assertiveness-training experience to assess and improve your assertion skills in a safe "laboratory" setting;[2] and *(c)* if needed, engage in some psychotherapy or spiritual direction to overcome any anger-based "residuals" that may inhibit your singling. (See chapter 11, "Where to Find Help.")

Here is a procedure I find most helpful when I am angry. It is not the only effective way to deal with anger, but it is one way. In outline form it goes like this:[3]

1. *Admit* to yourself that you are angry.
2. *Express* your anger in a safe environment to boil it down to its essence, clarify it, and defuse it.
3. *Restore* to conscious awareness your own attitude of love, without waiting for your adversary to change.
4. *Report* openly and directly the angry feelings you are experiencing.
5. *Negotiate* mutuality regarding the issue(s) at stake.

Admit, Express, Restore, Report, Negotiate. Let us examine this five-step model with an eye toward handling angry feelings that typify the singling process.

Admit it. It is often difficult for people to "own" their angry feelings, even if they believe that everyone has such feelings from time to time. Many of us have been reared in an environment where anger was not permitted. Valerie typified this in a singles sharing group:

> My parents weren't religious but they prided themselves on being upright and moral and mature. No one was ever allowed to raise his or her voice in our home. I think my mom and dad did argue on occasion, but always behind closed doors; so I never learned how to fight. When I got married to someone who turned out to be a very angry young man, it threw me. I didn't know what to do. It isn't that I was taught anger was wrong, exactly; just that it was, well, childish.

Such childhood learnings are common. They render conflict management a thorny task in adult life. Usually, "peace at any price" persons do not begin to deal with anger at all unless it becomes absolutely necessary because their singling is at stake. Even then, they'd rather not—but, like Valerie, they may recognize that denying their anger no longer serves them:

> I can see that my not knowing how to fight and being scared to try . . . well, it messed up my marriage for sure. I don't mean he didn't do his half of the messing up; he did. But my dissolving into tears, falling silent and retreating into the spare bedroom with a book for three days at a time . . . didn't help. . . . Just being able to sit here and admit to all of you that I am an angry woman is a giant step for me.

Some people, especially in religious families, are even more strongly indoctrinated; they are taught that anger is *wrong.* They may be surprised to hear Paul's admonition to the early Christian church: "Be angry but do not sin; do not let the sun go down on your anger" (Eph. 4:26). The apostle is clearly saying that the "sin" is not in having anger, but in harboring it—going to bed mad. People have far more control over their attitudes and actions than over their emotions. Since one's emotions are spontaneous, it is quite useless to deny their presence or substance. Feelings simply are. Therefore, one is wise, whenever anger comes, to admit it is there: "I am angry."

Express it. Once your anger is acknowledged, it is helpful to do something active to discharge it. Done in private or possibly in the company of a trusted confidant, this can help you boil down the anger to its essentials. Anger often has an unfocused, all-consuming character which is not helpful. In safe surroundings, do what will help you express it, refine or define it, and defuse it.

Different tactics work for different people: repeating an angry exclamation over and over again aloud; shouting; kicking some object harmlessly (an empty cardboard box will do); pounding on a pillow; carrying on a heated make-believe fight with one's "foe"; quietly conducting a more rational debate; or writing it all down on a piece of paper—all these methods have been successful. The idea is to pinpoint what it is you are feeling and at whom or what the anger is targeted, and to lessen its destructive potential by disarming its explosive core.

Once the anger has been admitted and expressed, its emotional heat will subside. One can then freely and deliberately proceed to the next step.

Restore your loving attitude. Allen, a singling father in a "Parents Without Partners" group, was talking about his constant battles with his son.

> I get so damn mad at that kid! It's funny; I never get that mad at anybody else. My boss can be totally unreasonable or the neighbors' kids can act like the worst brats in the world, but I never get mad at them. Yet I get so mad at Kirby I could kill him!

Of course. Allen had a love relationship with Kirby of unique consequence to him—a relationship that mattered so much it could trigger intense anger. Perhaps he saw himself in his son and was expecting more than a reasonable degree of perfection.

Maybe he was taking out his divorce-related frustration on Kirby. Maybe he was angrily afraid his son might reject him as his wife had. Maybe Kirby was indeed siding with his mother. Who knows? The interpretative possibilities are many, and only Allen and Kirby could figure it out, together. At the above moment in time, what Allen needed from the group was not speculation or advice but active listening. Fortunately, that's what he got.

The fact that anger comes automatically as a person's reflexive emotional reaction to feelings of rejection explains why singling people are often angry people. Especially if they have been deserted, divorced, or shabbily treated, singling persons may have experienced considerably more than their fair share of rejection—definitely more than non-singles, who are apt to be rewarded for hiding whatever rejection they feel. Singlers often feel so overwhelmed by rejection that they can no longer deny the anger it spawns.

One can sympathize with this, but if in the process of singling you find yourself functioning reflexively and defensively out of anger, you are in trouble. You are in trouble because you have lost your perspective of love, which is the only perspective from which one can successfully handle anger. You are not being angry lovingly . . . and nothing else works.

Instead, you are probably demanding that others behave pleasantly as a condition for your loving them or behaving decently toward them; and so you are in fact refusing to change your own hostile attitudes until others measure up to your expectations. Again, one can sympathize with this, but the trouble is it won't get you where you want to go. As one angry woman put it rather dramatically in a singles therapy group:

> I know if I keep this up I'm doomed to live my life as a basically bitchy, witchy, pissed-off person. I used to think I just couldn't help it, that it's just the way I am. But I don't believe that anymore. What I'm thinking now is that I must get some sort of perverse jollies out of being so angry all the time.
>
> If I don't, why do I keep it up?

If you are singling and angry, the good news is that you are by no means the helpless victim of your feelings. If anything has you under its spell, it is not your feelings but your *perceptions.*

People's feelings (whatever they are) are entirely dependent on the way they perceive their life situation. That perception, or attitudinal stance, can be softened by bringing back into focus "lost facts," such as the precious nature of human beings no matter what their performance.

For example, let's admit that you *perceived* your ex as precious and beloved enough for you to marry that person and bear children together. Let's say there's been utterly substandard performance of late—infidelity, fiscal irresponsibility, neglect of the children, whatever—strictly "D minus" performance. Is your ex not still a precious person? Hurting, obviously, but then so are you. You once perceived your ex as precious. Can you now still do so, not to remarry your ex or approve of the irresponsible behavior, but simply to pave the way for a successful negotiation so you won't both come out angry losers again?

The idea is not to repress any remaining anger, but to self-consciously restore one's attitude of love. In the case of the angry father Allen, he certainly needed to admit and express his anger, but then he needed to bring back to conscious awareness the preciousness of his son, Kirby, the fact of how very much Kirby meant to him. Allen loved Kirby.

The restoration of an attitude of love is absolutely necessary to the creative handling of anger. In such an attitude a person is free to choose how, then, to handle the anger. If you find this third step impossible, seek help.

Report it. To say, simply and openly and directly, "I am angry," or "I have a bone to pick with you," can be incredibly difficult. There are all kinds of reasons why this is so—pride, habit, nonassertiveness, discomfort with conflict, and unwillingness to admit one's angry feelings, to name a few. But delivering the "I am angry" message must be done—and as soon as possible, so that the relationship can be renegotiated and maybe even maintained on a more aboveboard basis than before. Who wants a relationship that is forever "on the outs"? To co-parent children or deal with money matters in such a relationship is hell on earth.

Admitting one's anger to oneself helps. Expressing and

defusing it privately helps some more. Restoring one's attitude of love for the other person helps more yet. Once that attitude is regained, the angry feelings have lost their power to control and the reporting can be done in a defensiveless, matter-of-fact manner that is disarming and paves the way for reasonable negotiation. Quietly, calmly, even peaceably one can say: "I am angry. May we please talk?"

The more people practice this fourth step, the more skill they develop in using it. It is an invaluable singling skill that will keep you from a lot of painful trouble and get you out of trouble when trouble comes. But for most of us, reporting anger never gets easy. My stomach always does a contortionist's dance. It helps to remember that I do it because I *care* about a relationship.

The question may arise, "What if my anger is toward an ex with whom I have no contact? What if she or he won't talk with me? Or what if she or he is deceased?"

There are ways. For instance, one can report one's anger to someone sitting, in the imagination, in an empty chair! But this is very difficult to do without help. If this is your dilemma, you may want to seek an assist from a skilled counselor.

Negotiate defensivelessly. Maturity is the art of defensivelessness, according to psychiatrist W. W. Broadbent.[4] "Defensiveless negotiating" is simply an active encounter within the context of an attitude of love. Two or more persons face an issue over which they have conflict and work it through because their relationship is important, and because they are aware that the best interests of each of them can only be achieved through careful attention to the best interests of both of them (or all of them). In this manner, what began as spontaneous anger becomes the catalyst for healthy relating. To illustrate, imagine the following conversation between the angry father mentioned earlier and his son, an eighth-grader:

ALLEN: I've felt a lot of anger toward you lately.

KIRBY: I know. I can tell.

ALLEN: Well, I want to talk about it. I've been doing a lot of thinking, about how important you are—how much you mean to me.

KIRBY: (*Quietly*) But you left us. (*Fighting back tears*)

ALLEN: Yes. Your mother and I chose not to live together anymore, and I agreed to be the one to move to another apartment. I didn't ever want to leave *you.*

KIRBY: I guess I thought maybe . . . maybe if I had just tried harder, you and Mom wouldn't have had to . . . I've been mad at her all the time ever since you left.

ALLEN: I didn't know that. All I knew is that you've been mad at me. Now I know that most of all you've been mad at yourself, huh?

KIRBY: Yeah.

ALLEN: Nothing you did caused the divorce. And it wasn't anything you failed to do. (*Pause*) I have more time for us now, more time for you and me. Let's figure out together how we want to use our time. OK?

KIRBY: OK. Can we go fishing?

Singles need to know how to "do" relationships, since no one else will do relationships for them. Since mutuality is the key to a healthy relationship, defensiveless negotiating of mutuality is the crucial singling skill for gaining, maintaining, or restoring relationships of all kinds.

Even so, while no demands can be legitimately made on another as a condition for loving that person, lots of legitimate demands can (and indeed must) be made as a condition for living or doing business with another. This is true in love, work, and play. However, *it is impossible to negotiate successfully when unresolved anger stands in the way.*

8

Men, Women, and Singling

In working with singling adults, I have met several times as many women as I have men. The ratio has been about four to one, even though I always try to recruit as many men as possible for a workshop or a series of interviews. Consequently, I have more data from singling women than from singling men. From my experience it seems that women are way ahead of men in learning singling.

However, I have learned a great deal about men too. In this chapter I will share some perspectives for women who want to understand men better and for men who, like Greg, may have a tough row to hoe on the singling way.

> Greg Walker phoned his minister in the middle of the night: "Reverend Jones, I hate to bother you but . . . (*Sobbing*) I just don't think I'm going to make it. I've been crying all night. I can't sleep. I can't even eat."
>
> Howard Jones thought quickly. "Can you meet me at eight o'clock in the coffee shop across from the church?"
>
> "Yes, I'll be there."
>
> "Good. Try to get some rest and I'll see you at eight."
>
> Greg was a handsome, athletic, thirty-five-year-old member of the church. He had a good education and a high-paying job. Why, wondered the pastor, was he so distraught? Then Howard remembered: Dottie, the woman who had been accompanying Greg to church, was missing last Sunday—Greg had sat alone. Could that be it?

> It was. At breakfast Greg told the pastor that he had asked Dottie to marry him and that her response had been to break off the relationship. Recently divorced, Greg was having difficulty surviving on his own. He was desperately seeking a new Mrs. Walker. Greg agreed to meet with Howard regularly for the next six weeks to talk about some ways to survive without getting married.[1]

Greg's story, told by his minister, is dramatic but not unusual. My own story is different from Greg's, but like him I found singling very difficult. I think most men do, and I suspect women do too.

Men, Women, and Reality

The experiences of singling women and singling men in our society show some characteristic differences, one of which is that women are more in touch with cultural and relational realities than men. This is not because of their femaleness, but because of the double standard and sexism of our culture.

Because of these cultural factors, singling women often experience a greater diminishing of their self-esteem than do their male counterparts.[2] It is implied, or they may be flatly told, that in their singlehood women are double or triple failures: They have failed to prove themselves sexually attractive; they have been inadequate wives, homemakers, and mothers, the traditional badges of femininity; and they have probably not advanced as far as they might have in their professional careers either—at least not in comparison with men of the same age.

In these and other ways, singling women in our society face a far more judgmental "put-down" than singling men.

Myths

Singling persons of either sex, especially when they feel hurt, angry, or insecure, sometimes accept certain pervasive but false notions that need to be corrected. Often these are learnings or yearnings from childhood that reassert themselves. The myths include:

- Men are independent, women are dependent.
- Men are sexual, women are spiritual.
- Men are stronger than women.
- Men are logical, while women are emotional.
- Men are forthright and trustworthy, while women are apt to gossip or lie (about their age, for example).
- Men are smarter than women. (Aren't the world's greatest scientists, entrepreneurs, scholars, and statesmen men?)
- There is a "natural order" to things, and males should be older, tougher, and more experienced in sexual matters and other "ways of the world" than their female counterparts.

Well, not only should such myths be flatly debunked, but the truth may be the exact opposite of what these "big lies" assert! It is an understatement to affirm that the above list would be just as accurate if it read:

- Women are independent, men are dependent.
- Women are sexual, men are spiritual.
- Women are stronger than men.
- Women are logical, while men are emotional.
- Women are forthright and trustworthy, while men are apt to gossip or lie (about their height, for example).
- Women are smarter than men. (Aren't the world's greatest lovers, friends, creative minds, and world leaders women?)
- There is a "natural order" to things, and females should be older, tougher, and more experienced in sexual matters and other "ways of the world" than their male counterparts.

Reversing the list is not only fun, but also revealing. My counseling experience suggests that in some substantial ways singling women are clearly more independent, more rational, more honest about themselves and their situations, and just plain stronger than singling men.

My own awareness began when I was interviewing a considerable number of separated spouses who were under the care of therapists. This research disclosed not only similarities but also some striking differences between the husbands and the wives:

- The women tended toward elation in their separation, while the men tended toward depression.
- The women found it easier to lean on others than did the men.
- There was a strong tendency for separated men to make changes in their sexual behavior (more masturbation, for instance, and more seeking after sex partners), while the women reported no change.
- Men increased significantly the time and energy they expended on household and personal maintenance tasks, while women took on few, if any, new tasks. (One woman thought and thought and finally volunteered, "Well, he did used to take out the garbage.")
- Separated husbands admitted to a higher degree of general anxiety than did separated wives.
- Finally, men reported diminished physical well-being and deterioration in such habits as eating, smoking, and drinking; women did not.[3]

Women consistently emerged in that study as anything but the "weaker sex."

Sexuality, Intimacy, and the Sexes[4]

Men are more prone to locate their sexual feelings in their genitals than are women. This may be because of the externality of male genitals, early and frequent masturbation which reinforces a genital focus, or the unexpected erections during adolescence which lead males to believe that their genitals are different from the rest of themselves.

Whatever the reasons, men seem to develop an *instrumental* view of sexuality which isolates sex from other areas of life, focuses the meaning of sexuality in the genital experience (the sex "act"), and brings them into adulthood seeing their genitals as important to both their masculine self-image and their views of the world.

It is as if men are supposed to penetrate, grasp, conquer, and possess whatever piece of the world may be theirs to capture. In the male world of achievement, it is hardness, upness, and straightness that are prized. Hard facts mean more than soft data; computers and other machines are "up" when they are functioning and "down" when they are not; and linear history is more important than the cyclical movements of nature, whether in a man's professional career or personal life.

With rare exceptions, as children we were all nurtured by women, usually our mother. She was our primary caregiver. Naturally, then, female children identify themselves as *like* mother, continuous with her, and their gender identity flows from her. Male children, on the other hand, from an early age begin to see themselves as *over against* mother, *un*like her, and needing to separate from her in order to establish their gender identity. They are taught to push away from the caregiver and to find out what masculinity is by *dis*identifying themselves from what it is not: "Boys are not girls; boys are not sissies; boys are not soft; big boys don't cry; big boys don't run to Mommy for comfort."

The Male Identity Trap

What does it mean, then, to be a man? When I interviewed Miles, I met a "real man" in the most traditional sense of the word.

> I think I was born with blue booties on. In my parents' house hangs a picture of me as an infant hugging a full-size football. My dad is a mechanical engineer, and very early on I got Lincoln Logs, Tinkertoys, and an Erector Set. My sisters got dolls and lots of miniature clothes, and coloring books and dance lessons. I remember my dad made them a huge dollhouse one Christmas; I got to help. They also got to cry, be scared, and sit in my father's lap. I was taught that was sissified behavior.
>
> By fifth or sixth grade I was into athletics—bodybuilding, Little League, and Pop Warner football. It was in junior high, the summer between seventh and eighth grades, that I cried for the last time. My dad gave me the belt for something and ordered me to stand there and take it like

> a man. When I started crying he said it was high time for me to quit acting like a crybaby; he said he'd have to keep hitting me with the strap till I stopped crying. He did, and I did, and I never cried again, ever.
>
> In high school I was a terrific achiever—all-conference three years in football, ninth in a graduating class of four hundred, went steady with the captain of the cheerleaders, and worked part-time at a hardware store, earning enough money to buy my own car before I turned seventeen.
>
> By the time I went off to college on a football scholarship, my masculine ego was very big. I was one aggressive dude. No one dared to cross me. And no one ever did . . . until last Christmas when Betty Ann took off for her folks' house in Atlanta with the kids and refused to come back.

Miles's story may be an extreme one, even a caricature, but it is true. It illustrates the way some males are oppressed (or repressed) in our society. Miles was carefully taught to do—to achieve, accomplish, put things together, compete, hang tough, win, succeed, make it in the world. He was not at all taught to be—to nurture, participate relationally, or show warmth, softness, caring, intimacy, or vulnerability.

As far as he was concerned, Miles had done everything a real man should do, and he had done it at an A-number-one level of excellence. He was respected for his accomplishments as an electrical engineer, he was earning a high salary, and he had endowed Betty Ann with "a quarter-of-a-million-dollar house and two of the most beautiful little kiddos you've ever seen!" What more could she possibly want? Oh, she had said several times that just once she'd like to see him cry, which was what brought him to therapy now. Maybe if he could cry for her he could get her back.

Miles was sad and angry to hear that learning to cry might take more than a couple of "lessons" and that the therapist could not present him with a precise "game plan." After two meetings with the therapist, he decided to find a way to get the job done more efficiently.

It is easy to see why someone like Miles is much more skilled at separateness and drawing boundaries than he is at the arts of intimacy, continuity, and friendship. Actually, he may also be at a loss when asked to define what it means to be a man. On the other hand, a woman can usually define what it means to be a woman, or at least what it means to her.

Further, singling demands androgyny. Androgyny as we see it means making friends with both the male and female aspects of ourselves. Whether we are heterosexual or homosexual, all of us are born with both masculine and feminine traits. Men tend to develop the former more, women the latter.

Androgyny means learning to befriend both our male and female aspects. The famous psychologist Carl Jung was the first to describe this. Jung called our masculine side the "animus" and our feminine side the "anima." He pointed out that *none of us is pure masculinity or pure femininity.* Each of us embodies both an animus and an anima.

The animus and anima are not primarily about sexuality. Rather, they have to do with our ability to embrace both the qualities that usually typify our own sex *and* those that usually typify the opposite sex. Whether we are sexually oriented to the opposite sex or to our same sex, we still have both femininity and masculinity. A simple example of androgynous behavior is a woman feeling free to ask a man for a date, or invite him along on a business trip simply for the pleasure of his company, or send him flowers on his birthday.

The singling task is to achieve balanced wholeness. A woman must learn to develop and embrace the maleness within her in balance with her femaleness. A man must learn to develop and embrace the femaleness within him in balance with his maleness. Androgynous singles are those men and women whose personalities and behaviors include a balanced mix of traits traditionally ascribed to one sex or the other, such as sensitivity (usually more visible in women) and assertiveness (usually more visible in men). Researchers have concluded that androgynous people of both sexes make the best lovers—not the macho men or markedly feminine women. One must be highly flexible to be a loving person, say the experts, which is impossible for people whose personalities conform to rigid sex stereotypes.

Women are better at androgynous development than men, probably because they have needed to expand their "maleness" to survive in "a man's world."[5] Men tend to fight the development of their "femaleness," possibly because they usually control the power structures in our society and see no advantage to giving up the superiority they assume is their male birthright. Also, many men associate their underdeveloped "soft side" with their fear of homosexuality. So irrational is their fear (homophobia) that they bend over backward to deny any hint of feminine qualities. Vulnerability, emotionality, artistic pursuits such as drama or dance, hands-on participation in the nurturing of children, and even careers in interior design or secretarial work are avoided. Many men view these as "women's things."

Therefore, with gradually more and more exceptions, the majority of men do not bother with singling. In the first place, they don't bother because *they don't feel the need to.* Today there still are plenty of non-single women who are shorter, sweeter, younger, poorer, and less educated than they and who are willing to submerge their identity into that of a big, brave, manly patron.

The second reason men don't bother with singling is that *they don't want to.* They already have the upper hand in society. Why give up their dominion?

And last but by no means least, men don't bother with singling because *they are afraid to.* Singling means getting back in touch with childlike fears, tears, and helplessness—feelings and vulnerabilities "real men" like Miles have been carefully taught to avoid and forget.

A Note to Women

So what's a woman to do, if she wants a man in her life? Partly tongue-in-cheek, but only partly, I would first say go slow in singling, carefully weighing the disadvantages of your growth toward maturity. Men will not grow up as much, as soon, or as often as women. The more wholly single you become, the less tolerant you will be toward male immaturity and the more threatening you will be to most men.

Second, if you are becoming fond of the freedom and power of singlehood and can no longer settle for less than an equal partnership, consider incorporating men into your life rather than "a man." Perhaps two or three men—let's say a friend, a professional colleague, and a playmate or lover—can collectively meet your desire for male presence in your life. In other words, find men who will enrich your life but not demand that you exclude all other men.

Third, if you seriously do your sexual homework and friendwork along the lines of chapters 9 and 10, you may find your intimacy and closeness needs well met. The result may be (1) a lifelong commitment to singlehood without any spouse at all, or possibly (2) a "pleasure bond" marriage with a man of whom you expect no more than he can deliver.

Consider Adriana, a successful entrepreneur who married a retired banker twenty-four years her senior.

Cecil, every inch a gentleman, adores Adriana and gladly accompanies her on business trips, to social functions, or on a shopping spree. He cheerily performs househusbandly chores responsibly and sees to routine matters such as maintenance of their automobiles. Cecil is not wealthy but is solvent, and he does not mind Adriana's earning a lot of money (which she does).

Cecil's children are grown and in scattered locations. Sometimes he goes to visit them and to be near his grandchildren for up to a month or more. He is balding, overweight, and less ambitious than Adriana. He also has a sweet spirit and is not at all possessive. Their marriage is sexual and monogamous, but both Adriana and Cecil were quite fully single when they met, and they remain single in many respects.

After watching this couple for several years, I am convinced that their relationship is mutually beneficial and warmly loving. I believe it will last until Cecil dies, leaving Adriana a widow—a probability they faced squarely before marrying.

On the other hand, for today's woman, there are compelling reasons why singlehood is more possible and desirable than ever before. Urbanization, overpopulation, and long lifespans have rendered marriage and childbearing less crucial for personal survival (and the survival of humankind). Adult education and career development are now possible and normative for women of any age, and often easier for singles than for marrieds. And a woman will not find herself an outcast, because many of her sisters are choosing permanent singlehood as the most healthful way for them to live in a predominantly sexist society. Historically, marriage has never been as good a deal for women as it has for men, anyway.[6]

9

Friendship and Singling

With some hesitancy, I use my own case in this chapter. The reason is that none of the men interviewed for this study, and relatively few of the women, spoke of the making of friends as a function of their singling process. I find that sad, because singling cannot be done without friendships.

> I had childhood and adolescent buddies, but I was past thirty before I discovered friendship. It was at about the same time that I began singling, and I cannot say which came first. Actually, I do not think I could have become single without my friends, which puts "friendwork," as I like to call it, among my most treasured skills.
>
> The first time I ever asked for friendship was in the middle of a rainy night, without even the courtesy of a phone call in advance. When Terry opened his door, bleary-eyed, all I could do was burst into tears and blurt out, "I need a friend!"
>
> Thank God, Terry didn't turn me out. Instead he pulled me inside, hugged me, made a pot of coffee, sat up with me, and listened, and I do mean listened, for hours. When his wife got up to get ready for work, Terry made us all breakfast so Judy could sit with me for a while too. Then, having convinced me to take the day off, Terry called in "sick" just to be available in case I needed him during the day. I will never forget it. Even though we now live far apart, I will always love Terry.

An only child and rather a loner by nature, I have found nothing matters more to me now than my friends—some far away and seen intermittently, but always a precious few locally.

What Friendship Is

A friendship is above all an *intimate* relationship, closely personal, deep, open, loving. Pursuing romance is easy, but the pursuit of intimacy is not. It is effortful.

A person may go through life never intimate with anyone—not with a parent, not with a sibling, and not with a spouse (whether the person has one spouse for fifty years or several spouses for several years each).

Men, in particular, often have marriages in which their wives are outsiders to the wheeling and dealing they, as husbands, live and die for. They may disclose more with business associates, but are these relationships friendships? Hardly. They are arrangements. It is commendable that on a battlefield men will die for comrades they hardly know. But friendship is different from that.

I like what Sam Keen says about friendship:

> Friendship exists as a sanctuary that is situated between the private world of the family, the ambiguities of sexual love, and the public world. . . . Friendship is a sanctuary precisely because within it we may be more than, and different from, the destiny we must wrestle with in the family or the roles we must assume to enter the contractual order of civility. With my friend I am neither [parent], nor merchant, nor citizen. I am uniquely myself. The value of friendship lies in its exemption from the rules of usefulness. . . . With my friend I may share my asocial, heretical, treasonous, antisocial, tabooed, or outrageous ideas, visions, and feelings.
>
> Friendship also sets us free, for a moment, from the sweet burden of sexuality.[1]

One of the most frequent complaints of singling women is that while men may want them as sexual lovers, men do not want them as friends. The reason is that few men know how to befriend.

In *The Hazards of Being Male,* Herb Goldberg illustrates men's plight with a touching story:

> While preparing this chapter [on friendship] I kept thinking back to a . . . seminar on aggression in which I participated. An actress conducted an evening program on the subject of aggression and the theatre.
>
> She arrived early in the afternoon . . . with a woman friend approximately her age who was helping her prepare for the evening presentation. Both are attractive, equally successful heterosexual women, and their friendship and interaction was very special to watch. [The actress's] friend hovered around her constantly, as involved and concerned that everything should be set up artistically and correctly as if the program was hers. She soothed and comforted the actress whenever she expressed any doubts or anxiety. . . . Then she helped her dress in an elaborate outfit, checking carefully to see that the make-up and the overall look were just right.
>
> Forty-five minutes before the program was to begin she urged her to rest up and volunteered to get everyone seated and to inform them that there would be no smoking. Once it began she was there . . . to help keep the program moving, and after it was all over she embraced her friend, helped her gather all the materials together and put them into the van. . . . Even though the woman friend was married and had children, she never expressed a feeling of being imposed upon nor rushed to get back home.
>
> As I observed this interaction go on for seven or eight hours *I was deeply moved, jealous and saddened at the same time. The jealousy and sadness I felt was for myself and for many other men who I believe rarely, if ever, are capable of or experience such a caring, sharing, and loving relationship . . .* one in which great pleasure is taken in facilitating the accomplishment of the other, just as if it were happening to oneself.[2]

The Imperative of Friendship

To become single we must learn to be and live alone, but few among us can bear to remain all by ourselves for extended periods. It does not follow, however, that we are necessarily meant to marry. Rather, we are meant to have in our lives at least one meaningful, intimate relationship. The model for such a relationship is not erotic love but friendship, which rarely takes place within marriage or family relationships. It is more likely to happen between two people for whom there is no other relationship except the sacred bond made in the covenant of friendship. Note what Sam Keen writes:

> Wouldn't it be marvelous if our best friend could be our most passionate lover? But longtime experience testifies that it seldom works. . . . Nowadays, in the dark ages of friendship, husbands and wives, or lovers, often claim they are each other's best friends. But I suspect this signals more a decline in the fortunes of friendship than an advance in the fortunes of marriage. . . .
>
> When men and women lose the habit of friendship, they . . . follow the illusion of romantic love, or sell themselves to the company store, or surrender their uniqueness for security. . . . Friendship is the surest antidote we have to self-betrayal. . . .
>
> Our vastness and inexhaustibility can only be glimpsed when we are accepted by our friends without conditions, qualifications, ifs, ands, or buts, with warts, wrinkles, wounds, and, perhaps, halos.
>
> When [friendship] is strong enough, we need little else—besides bread and shelter.[3]

Types of Friendship

Obviously, then, a big singling task is learning how to make and keep the friends one wants, rather than being a Lone Ranger (even he had Tonto!) or somebody who simply processes whoever happens to show up.

Muriel James and Louis Savary offer three models of friendship. They use clear equations to depict the three basic ways in which people approach friendships:[4]

$$\tfrac{1}{2} + \tfrac{1}{2} = 1$$

$$1 + 1 = 1 + 1$$

and

$$1 + 1 = 1 + 1 + 1$$

The first is: $\tfrac{1}{2} + \tfrac{1}{2} = 1$. This model, like many people's picture of traditional marriage, suggests that we are truly incomplete without our other half. Therefore, friendship becomes a context in which two incomplete persons find wholeness. The $\frac{1}{2} + \frac{1}{2} = 1$ style is perfectly sketched in the song "People,"[5] popularized by Barbra Streisand. The song's idealistic claim: Anyone who needs people badly enough will be transformed from a half person to a whole person with no more hunger or thirst!

In contrast there is a second model: $1 + 1 = 1 + 1$. This model is implied in the well-known song of the Beatles, "A Little Help from My Friends."[6] In the song, you may recall, I may seek my friends' help, but not in such a way as to risk my individuality. Rather, I bring my uniqueness to your uniqueness and we bring out the best in each of our individual selves. Neither of us owes the other anything; we simply complement and enjoy each another: $1 + 1 = 1 + 1$.

All of us have had $\frac{1}{2} + \frac{1}{2} = 1$ relationships. Most of us have also known helpful $1 + 1 = 1 + 1$ relationships, "buddyships." However, a third model offers the most creative friendship option of all. The equation is: $1 + 1 = 1 + 1 + 1$. James and Savary call this a "third-self friendship." It happens when two people come together in such close intimacy that without losing their individuality or uniqueness, they bond in a way that produces another kind of "self" as their friendship takes on a quality of its own, a life of its own. To quote the authors,

> Two people, like two [musical] notes, [can] come together in such a way that, without losing their individualities, they form a new entity. . . .
>
> Building a third-self friendship is easier if the friends involved realize they are indeed creating something new and that it is one of the most important things people can do in life.[7]

The possibilities of a "third-self friendship" are communicated well by Paul Simon in the song made famous by his friend Art Garfunkel, "Bridge Over Troubled Water."[8] It's a great ode to $1 + 1 = 1 + 1 + 1$ friendship.

Friendship is the most important relationship that can exist between two human beings. Moreover, ultimately *it is friendship that is most capable of meeting our deepest needs for intimacy.*

Several conclusions follow.

First, a fully single person with just one fully single friend would not need a spouse to fill the friendship vacuum. Many people marry because they want a friend, not realizing that friendship does not automatically come with marriage.

Second, those marriages which are truly life-giving and which meet one's deep needs for intimacy are marriages where two single friends commit their lives to each other as husband and wife. Even then, there is a danger that marriage can breed possessiveness or jealousy between the partners.

Third, singles who master the art of friendship can lead the way in helping society learn to accept and validate friendships outside of marriage. Many people have intimacy needs that cannot be met by only one individual and that must be filled by friends other than one's spouse. A mistake newly married people commonly make is to "fire" their individual friends and begin to operate exclusively as a couple—in a $\frac{1}{2} + \frac{1}{2} = 1$ style, which is a non-single style.

Fourth, friendship, in and of itself, can be such a deeply satisfying intimate relationship that singles who have friends can become complete and fully whole persons whether or not they ever have a marriage partner.

How to Befriend

In recent years some good primers on friendship have been published, and anyone serious about singling should study them.[9] Here are a few recommendations you will find useful in beginning to get the friends you want.

First, *commit yourself to try satisfying your inner yearning for intimacy with friendship.* Give it a year. The worst that can happen is that *(a)* you learn a great deal, *(b)* you don't get your intimacy needs satisfied, and *(c)* next year you rechannel your energy into trying to find a romance. The best that can happen can be indescribably grand, last a lifetime, and leave you freer than ever to pursue romance. So what are you afraid of?

Probably two things: failure, and success.

What if you study friendship, hope and pray that you can make a friend, risk reaching out, and get rejected? It can happen. If it does, assess what happened, take in what you've learned from the experience, seek a consultant if you'd like, and try befriending someone else.

It may be that you chose an inappropriate person; or that person is overextended and has no room for a new friendship, or means well but is afraid of closeness, . . . or he or she has a possessive lover or spouse! Please do not give up on making a close friend till you've tried at least five or six different people who have the qualities you are seeking and who appeal to you. There are no guarantees, but it is scarcely possible that a singling adult could give a whole year to the enterprise and fail.

But what if you succeed? You may have to give up your "no touch" or "no touch unless it's sexual" existence. You may have to face sexual phobias and make peace with genuinely loving a same-sex person. This is a particularly difficult hurdle for some men, who need to learn to distinguish intimacy needs from genital needs. You may even have to face what others will think, or say, about you and your friend, be it a she or a he. Most of all, you may have to abandon your romantic fantasy of getting absolutely all your needs met by just one other human being, the perfect "10" of your dreams.

Second, *act.* Get intentional; get assertive. The best word for it is courtship, except that this time you are not courting a potential lover or spouse—you are courting a potential friend. If you need assertiveness training, get it. If you need the support of a singles group, find one. If you are paralyzed by fear, seek a therapist. But having committed yourself to friendwork, make a list of all those you think you might want to court, put the names in rank order, and act.

Third, *act locally.* Long-distance friends won't do. We live in an extremely mobile society; today's friend may live in Timbuktu tomorrow. Correspondence is slow; phone calls are expensive; and neither calls nor letters can substitute for presence. In one's time of need, one needs a local friend. I have met many singling wayfarers who spoke of their wonderful friends "back home"—and they are usually lonesome, vulnerable people who do not feel at home where they live. Long-distance friendships don't work any better than long-distance marriages.

Fourth, *try to make at least one friend of the same sex.* This is easier for most women than for most men. Read Lillian Rubin's *Just Friends.*[10] If you are male, read also Goldberg's *The Hazards of Being Male.*[11] Some additional suggestions are: Find someone, male or female, who has a close same-sex friend and talk with him or her about it; or find a therapist and schedule six sessions focused specifically on your own personal "friend-making project." A woman therapist is a good idea. Even if you are a man whose goal is a male friend, chances are a woman can help you overcome your homophobia or other fears more rapidly than her male counterpart. Chapter 11 will help you shop for an appropriate therapist or spiritual director.

There are some women who find it hard to be close to other women. Sometimes they also find it hard to be close to men without romantic and genital activity. If you are such a woman, find another woman as strong as you and as male-oriented as you, and befriend her. Or again, some focused therapy can help a lot.

Fifth, *try for at least one friend of the opposite sex.* This can get tricky, but it is well worth your best effort. My women friends enrich my life immeasurably. Women bring me perspectives no man can, so I try always to have one woman friend in my life, a local phone call away. She is not my lover, ever; in fact, we discuss that possibility at our friendship's first bud and agree to rule it out. It helps if she and I are very different in age, or if she has a satisfying marriage. Befriending a female peer professional colleague works best for me personally.

Sixth, *woo and win the most desirable friend you can find,* someone at least as grown-up as you, who can contribute as much to you as you can to him or her. I am not speaking of social climbing. You'll want to avoid judging a person's value by outward appearances. But you'll never find a friend by looking for needful "losers" either.

When I made a thousand-mile move from Arizona to California, I bid a teary good-bye to the closest friends I'd ever had—men and women who had helped me weather a stormy divorce and tenderly but firmly challenged me to become single and stay that way.

I settled into my new home and job—and into loneliness. I

burned the long-distance telephone wires and used a couple of romances to cope, but I needed a friend at arm's length. After several false starts I found someone I truly wanted—a wise, deep, thoughtful man, a leader, a professional peer, but a private person with many commitments and a marriage to tend. I just knew he'd be too busy to take me on, but mustering all my courage, I asked him out to lunch. He accepted.

As the small talk played out and lunch was served, we both fell into silence. It was my move. Looking more at my plate than at him (not good technique at all, but I was embarrassed and afraid of rejection), I said softly, "I've been watching you from afar for some time. I like what I see. I am seeking a friend, and the reason for this lunch is to ask you to consider becoming my friend. I don't know how close we'd want to get or what form our friendship would take, but we could start now and see where it wants to go. If you can make time for an occasional meeting like this and are willing to try . . ." As my voice trailed off I looked up—to see him crying! He was lonely too. No one had ever approached him this way. He was touched. We became fast friends. What a great feeling!

Seventh, *consider firing some of your present "friends,"* even if it means hurting someone's feelings or making an enemy. Many people's lives are cluttered with casual social or business contacts or family members with whom they eat, play, and "hang out." By the time their working, parenting, and other obligations are added, there is no mealtime or evening left open for developing a friendship. Ask yourself: Are the people I have in my life the people I want in my life?

I find this question very difficult personally. I tend to be a workaholic, and the nature of my work is such that it is often smart to entertain, be entertained, or attend gatherings for the school's sake or career purposes. I have painfully concluded that *(a)* I alone can control my time—no one will do it for me; and *(b)* I may not be able to determine how and with whom I spend professional time, but I always have a choice about how and with whom I use personal time.

Each of us gets exactly 168 hours each week. Even if one spends sixty or seventy hours doing professional "work," what about the remainder of the time that is left after sleeping and other personal matters? How many hours each week will you budget for the express purpose of friendwork?

Eighth, remember that *friendship is more art than science.* You may master techniques, but without artistry and soul you will come across as hollow or manipulative. To become a whole single, one must become an artist, a master friend maker.

Studies by sociologists, industrial psychologists, and career counselors of all the people fired from jobs show that social incompetence accounts for 80 to 85 percent of the discharges. Only about 15 percent are due to technical incompetence. The better your social skills, the better your life will go. The art of making a lifelong friend is the consummate social skill—much more difficult than getting someone into bed or to the marriage altar.

Jody was a tiny, winsome woman from the Midwest. We met at a singles conference where, as a conference leader, I did some informal counseling with her in the wake of her divorce. She was scared, lonesome, far from home, and longing for relief from her pain. She desperately wanted to find a man and to remarry.

I pleaded with her to go slow and make some friends first. We corresponded occasionally. Her letters showed steady growth. Three years after our only face-to-face meeting, she summarized her learnings:

> I have learned a great deal about marriage during this unmarried time. I want to learn all I can know. I want to know what marriage is in today's world, and why it is what it is, and how to tell when it might work and when it might not. And I want to know (I know living is taking risks) what to do about it—shy of another formal ceremony destined to end in another (ugh) divorce. I know my failure in marriage left me traumatized and gun-shy, but that has been a blessing. I'm still single (hooray) and I've learned so much. Anyway, with the help of therapy and the caring friends I have made, I think most of the fears are behind me now.
>
> The past couple of years I feel as if I've had a series of increasingly successful relationships, like mini-marriages;

> and I truly am open now to the possibility of a permanent relationship. But I don't have to have one (hooray). I want to be well married to me, first. Then *I want to keep learning how to be well married to my friends* (the women and men who've become so precious to me), second. And then maybe, just maybe, I'll be free to (and will want to) choose to get well married to one special person . . . third.

Jody's letter still thrills me. As she established, deepened, and relied on friendships, she grew up into a beautiful single adult.

Finally, *covet and cultivate the spiritual gift of love.* Leo Buscaglia is a contemporary who has devoted his life to the study of love, and his books are worth scanning. If you are a man, you may need to learn how to love a woman without acting sexual, or how to love another man without fearing homosexuality. If you are a woman, you may need to learn how to differentiate love from romance, or how to love someone without giving your power away to that person. Whatever your need, studying love and practicing friendship can help.

Paul started with as great a love deficit as anyone in history. But once apprehended and befriended,[12] he wrote of love as eloquently as anyone in history:

> Love is patient; love is kind and envies no one. Love is never boastful, nor conceited, nor rude; never selfish, not quick to take offense. Love keeps no score of wrongs; does not gloat over other [people's] sins, but delights in the truth. There is nothing love cannot face; there is no limit to its faith, its hope, and its endurance. . . . There are three things that last for ever: faith, hope, and love; but the greatest of them all is love.
>
> 1 Corinthians 13:4–7, 13, NEB

As you learn to befriend, then, ponder this: *The pursuit of sex or romance is neither the way to love nor the way to singlehood. The pursuit of friendship is the way to both love and singlehood.* It is also the path to wholeness.

10

Sex and Singling

Francine's and Mona's stories illustrate the extremes today's singles face in the area of sex. Most will fall somewhere between the extremes, but the dilemma is real. Let Francine go first.

> You asked me to talk about sex. That's not easy, but I'll try. Where should I begin?
>
> (INTERVIEWER: Wherever you'd like.)
>
> OK. I had a rocky start.
>
> I was a virgin and Dick was too. He was barely eighteen, I was still sixteen. We thought we were Romeo and Juliet. He graduated from high school Friday night and we got married Saturday night. I'll never forget that Saturday night. He hadn't made a reservation anyplace until Sunday night, so we drove for hours in the rain to find a motel. Both of us had chest colds, and when we finally got a room we were as exhausted as we were nervous. We wanted to consummate the marriage, but I was too dry and Dick was too impatient. He decided we needed a lubricant, so we used the only lubricant either of us had—Vicks Vaporub. (Laughs) It's funny now, but it wasn't then; both of us ended up screaming in the shower.
>
> When we went for marriage counseling twenty years later, our counselor asked me whether Dick was a good lover. The only way I could think to answer her was "Compared to whom?"

Now I'm almost fifty years of age . . . what am I supposed to do now about sex? The guys and gals at work tell me I'm attractive, that I should go out—they keep wanting to "fix me up." And I would like to have some fun. You know, Dick's funeral was two years ago. . . . But how can I tell my friends the reason I won't go out on a date is I'm scared to death of sex!

Here is Mona's story:

I'm forty but I still feel eighteen in so many ways. One of them is sex. I just plain like it. I like as much as I can get without prostituting myself. I don't like labels, but I've been called a nymphomaniac a few times. I don't care. I don't think it's possible to be oversexed. I think most people are undersexed, if you want to know the truth about it.

Trouble is, while I'm good at "getting myself off," I just plain like men. Even if I'm just using a vibrator on myself I'd rather do it with a man than all by myself. *(Laughs)* I guess that makes me some kind of exhibitionist too? *(Laughs again)* Well, OK. So be it. *(Pause)*

(INTERVIEWER: You said "Trouble is." I'm wondering what you mean by "trouble.")

Well, the trouble is I keep getting myself into trouble. I've been married and divorced twice, but there really was a third one in between the other two. Serious enough for me to move to California with him. And he would've married me. But when my ex bribed our son into living with him and threatened that I'd never see my only child again, I panicked and moved back to where they lived. Of course there've been lots of other men . . . during my marriages, in between marriages, and since. But nobody I wanted for the duration except those three; and I left all three of them, partly because they were into their careers too much and, frankly, I wanted more sex than any one of them could give me.

How does a singling adult deal with sex in a healthy way? A physically, mentally, emotionally, spiritually, and morally healthy way?

Hundreds of books have been written about sex and human sexuality. Some of the more useful ones are included in the list "For Further Reading" at the back of the book. Your singling time is an opportune time to become intimately familiar with your own sexual makeup and to learn to fulfill your own sexual needs. It is also important that singling men learn all they can about female sexuality, and that singling women learn all they can about about male sexuality. This knowledge can "defuse the mine" of fear about the opposite sex and help you become a better lover when the time is right.

Sexual Singling Is Important

Just as all of us are physical, intellectual, emotional, interpersonal, and spiritual beings, each of us is also a sexual being. To put it another way, sex is a natural function.

It is possible to control natural functions such as breathing, digesting, or elimination for periods of time, but we cannot suppress them altogether. Some people who rigorously discipline themselves for religious or other reasons may be able to control sexual functioning for an extended period of time, even for a lifetime. I admire them. There is a place for sexual celibacy. Some singles have embraced it as their path to wholeness.[1] (We will discuss this more a little later.) For most of us, however, it is an almost impossible and unnatural behavior. So strong is one's sexual way of being that when a child is born, if he is a boy, within his first twenty-four hours of life he will have an involuntary erection. If she is a girl, within her first twenty-four hours she will experience involuntary vaginal lubrication.

When was the last time you had a sexual experience? Probably pretty recently. We all have sexual experiences on an everyday basis. We may not always be aware we are having them, but no relationship is devoid of sexual overtones, whether there is any overt sexual behavior or not. This being so, legal-institutional marriage is certainly not and cannot be the only context for proper sexual expression.

A widow, whose husband had died suddenly, said to me, "Is it really God's will that I should have no sexual pleasure for the rest of my life? I am willing to consider remarriage but have found no opportunity. I do not want to be promiscuous, and I was raised to be a good Christian, but I am a sexual creature and I need sexual expression." Indeed she does. So do we all.

Sex and Sexuality

Learning to understand and express one's sexuality does not necessarily mean, or lead to, penile-vaginal intercourse. The idea that it must, or even should, is one of the sad myths of our performance-oriented Western culture. To illustrate, a physically handicapped person can most certainly "make love" meaningfully. Glenn and Joy, a married couple I know, were devastated by an auto accident that left Glenn permanently paralyzed from the waist down. Says Joy, "I'd rather have Glenn's lips and hands and words loving me than all the penises I can imagine."

Briefly, let's distinguish between sexuality and sex. Strictly speaking, sex is activity, while sexuality is a life condition, a basic ingredient in being human. From the moment of birth everyone has a plentiful interest in sexuality. Unfortunately many men and some women, having bought into the philosophies of Hugh Hefner (*Playboy*), Bob Guccione (*Penthouse*), and other high priests of pleasure-seeking and male domination (or female domination, as in *Playgirl* and elsewhere), think the focus of sexuality is on sex—on "scoring" or even on sexual athletics where "good sex" becomes something like simultaneous grand mal seizures while performing on a trampoline.

To be as clear as possible: In no way do I put down sex as such. At its best, under the best conditions, sex can be healthy cooperation (doing *with* someone), healthy complementarity (doing *for* someone), or even healthy competition (doing *to* someone). But one man I interviewed explained to me that life, for him, is finding the perfect sex partner, which is "just like buying a food processor":

> Let's say there's a dozen to choose from and you can have any one you want but once you've bought it you have to keep it for a long time, maybe even the rest of your

> life—like you're stuck with it, or it sure would cost you an arm and a leg to get rid of it, if you know what I mean? . . . Well, anyway, you sure wouldn't want to buy one of 'em without doing a lot of research, and the best way to do your research would be to try 'em all out—try each of 'em in your own kitchen for a month.

Yes, the man was serious. And of course, nothing could be further from the truth.

Yet even in our enlightened society single sexuality is generally spoken of as "premarital sex." Because sex is a natural function, because all relationships are naturally sexual, and because there is so much falsehood, the singling adult must get her or his thinking clear before venturing out into the sexual mine field.

What to Pursue

Five growth tasks are pertinent to sexual singling.

First, *become your own best lover.*

For several years I corresponded with a very special man in his fifties. I never actually met him, but we became friends by mail. A prominent minister in a major Protestant denomination, Nathan[2] never married, a situation that greatly troubled him for many years. The facet of nonmarried life that burdened him most was his sexuality. Nathan's sexuality became a serious focus for his singling journey during the years of our correspondence—so serious that he entered therapy to deal with it. His growth in the area of sexuality was phenomenal: it became a sun to light Nathan's singling path. From a letter:

> John, a strong change is taking place in my life. With the support of various persons, I am coming to accept myself much more than I did. By acceptance I mean accepting my total self.
>
> Marguerite [Nathan's therapist] suspects that I experienced child-molestation. Though I am not conscious of any specific incidents of sexual abuse, I shared with her some memorable events, such as being whipped by my

> mother with a stick with thorns, leaving my legs bleeding.
>
> But here's the big change: I accept my sexuality as it is! My sexual feelings are now a beautiful part of me that God loves and created. In my prayers I thank God for them and for the God-given gift of masturbation.
>
> Because of Cynthia [a single woman, not in his congregation, with whom Nathan became lovers for a brief time] I learned to appreciate, with a woman, our sexuality. Now, through the pain and hurt that came from that relationship, I have learned so very much about myself as a person. I have, with Cynthia's and Marguerite's help, come to accept my singlehood as a good and valid lifestyle (though others may not).
>
> In light of the deep-rooted anger, lack of trust, and hang-ups about sexuality I formerly felt, it has been a good thing (for at least two persons) that I did not marry earlier in life. It would have been a painful if not disastrous experience. If only I had known twenty-five years ago what I know now—but I didn't.

Nathan had rarely masturbated before, and never without guilt. He is now able to celebrate autoeroticism, becoming one's own best sexual lover, as one of the keys to successful singlehood. Masturbation is an invaluable singling skill.

Nathan is a rarity among men. Many men masturbate freely and frequently from an early age, and on into adult life, with little or no guilt. Far fewer women do so, and because some women have taken issue with my open emphasis on masturbation, it is important to explain its positive value.

When one considers the multitude of people who have entered into premature or unwise marriages to legitimate their hunger for sexual expression, the potential value of masturbation begins to become clear.

Many of us were brought up to believe masturbation is a no-no, so much so that "it is far easier to admit that one does not believe in God, or was once a Communist, or was born illegitimately, than that someone fondles a part of . . . [one's] own body to the point of orgastic release."[3]

Because it is so misunderstood, let's look for a moment at parental and religious prohibitions against masturbation. To quote one authority, a seminary professor:

> Millions of Christians masturbate, and do so with guilt and self-recrimination because they do not or cannot control themselves better.
>
> It's not a bad idea . . . to remind ourselves that self-love isn't a horrible, un-Christian thing. Most of us masturbate at one time or another in our lives, and, as a matter of fact, some believe this can be a safe sexual outlet for the divorced Christian—certainly one not nearly so destructive as the frenetic search for sexual encounters.[4]

The author goes on to say that with a right attitude one can express self-love, affirm God-given sensuality, and learn about oneself as a sexual person through masturbation. He continues that the Bible, which takes sexuality for granted, contains no proscription against autoeroticism; that is, there is no scriptural authority for our churches' traditional objections. On the contrary, the real biblical understanding of love includes self-love. Understanding this, we should rid ourselves of our guilt and concentrate instead on the possible usefulness of self-love, including sexual self-love:

> Women may have experienced orgasm rarely in sexual intercourse, and masturbation can help them learn methods which bring fuller sexual gratification. Most of us fantasize, and since self-love (as Jesus' commandment makes clear) is involved in love of others, it may be helpful to focus your fantasies on the tender, nurturing, and constructive aspects of love-making rather than on violent, manipulative, or destructive ones. Fantasies of sexual passion and vitality are not wrong.[5]

Another authority, eminent psychologist June Singer, writes that

> the physical pleasure and the release from tension that masturbation can bring about is only a minor part of what is involved. The fact that masturbation is so prevalent and that it is able to bring about an unfailing sensation of delight, or at least relief, proves that some important human need is being met by it. . . . From earliest childhood on into youth and maturity, masturbation is *an*

> *act of self-assertion, the object of which is a movement in the direction of independence.*[6]

Apart from sexuality as such, self-assertion and independence are two major singling skills a singling adult needs to develop or improve. Singer is clearly saying that masturbation can help. But she presses her analysis even farther:

> *There is great freedom in knowing that one can be whole in one's inner life, and that this wholeness need not depend absolutely upon a relationship with another person.* This is not to say that we should all prefer masturbation to sexual relations. What is most important is that *if one is open to . . . the value of masturbation, then a sexual relationship with another person becomes a matter of choice* rather than a matter of necessity. When the sexual relationship with another person does occur, it has the character of strength coming from the union of two independently potent individuals.[7]

I am aware that in the minds and hearts of many readers is the dream of marriage someday—of finding an appropriate partner and marrying, for living and for life. Remember: The primary prerequisite to being well married to another is first being well married to oneself. There are a lot of facets to being well married to oneself, but from the perspective of one's sexuality, masturbation is usually the best place to start, because it offers both immediate and long-term benefits.

For some, of course, masturbation is no issue; the skills are already in place and may need neither activation nor enhancement. Other issues are more pressing. But for others, it definitely is an issue. OK, you may ask. How do I start?

Somewhat paradoxically, the best way to begin incorporating masturbation into one's singling lifestyle is not learning and practicing totally in secret but with the support of a discussion group (such as a women's support group) or in individual psychotherapy, where one is free to candidly and honestly talk about the matter and express doubts, feelings, struggles, and successes.

When one is developing or mastering a skill, a teacher or coach and a support network is not only useful but may determine whether the results are favorable. This is why we have

Spanish teachers, voice coaches, tennis instructors, and sex educators. It is the best way to learn efficiently and effectively.

But reading about female (or male) sexuality can also help, and "bibliotherapy" may be where you need to begin because of geographical isolation or financial distress. You will find suggestions in the reading list.

Second, *get your sexual ethics clear.*

The time to say "Oh, my, I shouldn't be doing this" is not at midnight in the heat of passion in the apartment of someone you are dating. On the other hand, the time to say "If only I'd had the courage to show Pat how much I care" is not after Pat finally gave up on you after a year of trying to break through your armor-plated inhibitions.

The time of singling is the ideal time to discover what one believes, what one values, and what one truly wants. Without one's original family's constrictions or a spouse to consider, one can discern, discuss, experiment, or change one's mind rather freely.

In no area is this truer than in the area of sexual behaviors. Questions like: What do I dare risk? What do I want to try that I've never tried before? Where should I draw the line? How can I keep from violating my own sense of what is right? What about my children with their all-seeing eyes and all-hearing ears? What would my parents think? What will God think? What if I get hurt?—and many others including, How can I make sure I don't get AIDS or some other sexually transmitted disease?—spring forth as if they had a will of their own.

Do not decide in isolation. One is not a law unto oneself. Comes the basic question: To whom shall I go for counsel?

Again, as in the case of autoeroticism, there is excellent reading material. But reading about sexual ethics can be ponderous. It is hard to trust an author one has not met. And difficult ethical decisions must be worked through in the context of one's unique situation.

For these reasons, as a questing single I hope you consult at least one person whose authority you respect and whose wisdom you trust—your priest, minister, rabbi, or spiritual director; the wisest older person you know; a teacher who modeled mature womanhood or manhood for you; your therapist; or someone whose singlehood you admire. Once you've done so, get a second opinion.

There are three basic choice options in moral decision-making.[8]

1. The absolutist way: The law alone will determine my response in any given situation. Therefore, all I need is what the law says—my country's law, my parents' law, my church's law, or whatever law there is. Give me a code of ethics to follow and I shall adhere to it completely.

2. The existential way: I and I alone will determine my response in any given situation. I am the only "law" I need. Therefore, the world is regarded as my oyster and I look out for number one. *Caveat emptor*—let the "buyer" beware. My job is to be an astute "seller."

3. The contextual way: That which best serves humankind in love will determine my response in any given situation. Therefore, I will regard attitudes, decisions, and actions as immoral if they produce an increased distrust of people; deceit and duplicity in relationships; barriers between persons and groups; resistant, uncooperative attitudes; exploitative behavior toward others; diminished self-respect; or thwarted and dwarfed individual capacities.

On the other hand, I will deem attitudes, decisions, and actions moral if they produce an increased capacity to trust people; greater authenticity and integrity in relationships; a dissolving of barriers between persons and groups; cooperative attitudes; faith and confidence in people, enabling appropriate risk-taking; enhanced self-respect; and fulfillment of individual capacities or potentials.

Holly, a singling thirty-year-old with three daughters, did it right. Following her divorce, she joined a "Divorce Recovery" support group, did her grieving, and waited several months before accepting a date. She wanted to feel sure she wasn't dating out of sheer lonesomeness or looking for a rescuer. She wanted not to offend her daughters, who tended to be sympathetic toward their father, whom Holly had divorced when it became clear that he was gay. But most of all, she had married young and her husband "taught me all I knew, which wasn't much." In short, dating scared her. This proved a blessing, because it pushed Holly to read and study about love and sexuality. She reports:

> When I did start dating, was I ever glad I had my act more or less together! The first man I dated not only wanted to get me in bed on the first date; he wanted to marry me on the second date! He hadn't even spent five hours with me, or five minutes with my daughters.
>
> The next man I dated insisted that if I was to see him I couldn't see anybody else. And my third suitor tearfully explained to me that his ex-wife had left him just because he occasionally slept with other women—a weakness he was sure I could cure! I couldn't believe my ears.
>
> I was beginning to get discouraged but then Ben came into my life, and he was very different. From the start, he was a sensitive human being.
>
> I've been dating for a year now, and I have yet to do anything I regret. But I certainly am learning a lot about myself, and about men. By the way, Ben and I are still seeing each other. *(Holly is smiling.)*

Jim Nelson, a highly respected ethicist, has extensively considered the matter of sexual expression. Nelson sets forth three general principles that he regards as appropriate norms for decision-making.

Nelson's first principle is that love requires a single standard and not a double standard for sexual morality. Love must always be expressed as justice. Without justice it becomes individualistic and shallowly sentimental. Love expressed as justice becomes the lively concern for the empowerment of all persons, so that everyone has rightful access to the means for human fulfillment. This implies that there cannot be one sexual ethic for males and another for females, nor one for the unmarried and another for the married. The same basic considerations of love must be applied to everyone.

Next, Nelson says that the physical expression of one's sexuality with another person must be appropriate to the level of loving commitment present in that relationship. Our relationships exist on a continuum—from fleeting to lasting, from casual to intense, from relatively impersonal to deeply personal. So also physical expressions exist on a continuum—from varied types of eye contact and casual touch, to varied forms of embrace and kiss, to bodily caresses, to petting and foreplay, to various forms of sexual intercourse. In one way or another we inevitably express our sexuality in every human relationship, says Nelson. The morality of that expression will depend on its appropriateness to the shared level of commitment and the nature of the relationship itself.

Nelson's third principle is that genital sexual expression should be evaluated in regard to motivations, intentions, the nature of the act itself, and the consequences of the act, each of these informed and shaped by love.[9]

Following an elaboration of the several aspects of this third principle, Nelson adds:

> Some readers will want to lay claim to more specific sexual rules in addition to guiding principles such as these. If so, well and good. I personally find certain sexual rules important and useful. I do not view them as exceptionless absolutes, but I presume strongly in their favor, and the burden of proof is then on me to justify any exception by its greater faithfulness to the higher loyalty. Rules can protect us at the boundaries of our experience where we encounter our limitations in knowledge and wholeness. But however sexual rules are used, they should nurture our growth into greater maturity and responsible freedom, and not inhibit it.
>
> To love is to be open to life. Nowhere is this more evident than in the directly sexual forms of our loving.[10]

In singling sexually, a third growth task to pursue is to *explore your nonsexual options.*

There are alternatives to sexual activity. Everyone, single or non-single, experiences times of sexual tension. Let's suppose that because of moral commitments or geographical isolation, the options I am suggesting here are unworkable for you. Why not try some alternatives to sexual activity?

The best one may be to take your mind off yourself and your sexual hungers by becoming involved in others' concerns. Volunteer to work for social justice, tackle a major project you've put off, find a neighbor who needs a listening ear. The telephone company is onto a good idea when it advises us to "reach out and touch someone."

I dislike cold showers, but I've been told they help tame sexual hunger. I do know vigorous exercise helps. You might also try reading a book, attending a concert, or eating a gourmet meal in a good restaurant.

A friend who has been celibate for ten years told me she has learned to recognize the signs of strong sexual yearnings and to deal with them early, before they get to the stage where they dominate everything in her life. She calls her most specific yearning "skin hunger," the need to be touched. She has developed a network of friends at work and at church who are "safe to hug." Both she and her friends understand clearly that hugging is all that is on the agenda, that it is not any sort of prelude to deeper sexual involvement.

Fourth, *woo and win the people you want for your life.*

We discussed friendship in the previous chapter. But right now in the context of single sexuality, I must reiterate that until a singling adult knows how to make a friend and has an adequate support network of friends, she or he is scarcely ready for sexual espression with another person.

The reason for this is vulnerability. Karen Lebacqz, a seminary professor of Christian ethics, writes:

> Precisely because sexuality involves vulnerability, we [singles] need protective structures in the sexual arena. . . . The more sexual involvement there is to be, the more there needs to be a context that protects and safeguards that vulnerability so that its expression can be appropriate.
>
> Traditionally, monogamous marriage has been understood to be such an environment. Whatever the actual pitfalls and failures of marriage in practice, certainly in theory the commitment of a stable and monogamous marriage provides a supportive context for vulnerable expressions of the self. As Stanley Hauerwas puts it, " . . . Genuine love is so capable of destruction that we need a structure to sustain us."[11]

Lebacqz continues that, at its best, marriage provides such a structure. It ensures that the vulnerability of sexuality is private and that the sexual and other failures of the spousal pair remain protected within the context of a mutually vulnerable and committed relationship. She then says:

> Singleness carries no such protections. It is an "unsafe environment" for the expression of vulnerability. There is no covenant of fidelity to ensure that my vulnerability will not lead to my being hurt, foolish, exposed, wounded. In short, in singleness the vulnerability that naturally accompanies sexuality is also coupled with a vulnerability of context. Thus, singleness is an . . . explosive arena for the expression of vulnerability in sex because it lacks the protections of marriage. It heightens vulnerability.[12]

To be adequate, therefore, says Lebacqz, a sexual ethic for singles must provide what is needed in order for there to be appropriate vulnerability in sexuality. Unequal vulnerability is never appropriate. And in a culture where men tend to have more power than women and women are more vulnerable than men, great care must be taken to ensure an adequate context for the expression of single sexuality:

> *Single people will have to explore their own vulnerability to find its appropriate expression in sexuality.* Neither the "thou shalt not" of traditional prohibitions nor the "thou shalt" of contemporary culture provides an adequate sexual ethic for singles.[13]

For singling adults, the best context for the exploration of vulnerability is the context of friendship. For many it may even be the only context. Often one's childhood family is far away or not at all helpful. The aloneness of singling is often not just emotional but geographical. I have met many singles in San Francisco, Phoenix, Denver, or Topeka whose families and friends are "back home in Indiana." Going "home" may be impossible or undesirable because of work and other factors. One must develop a support network where one is—"bloom where you are planted," as the saying goes.

Let me define friendship in the context of single sexuality and vulnerability. A friend is someone who fully accepts you as you are, while at the same time challenging you to become all you can be, not for any benefit you can give the friend but solely for your benefit.

As you sort out the "how, why, when, and with whom" of sexual expression as a single, it may help to see one person's list of her friends. Deirdre calls this her "support system":

Marsha, my therapist
My eight "sisters and brothers" in the Tuesday evening "Suddenly Single" growth group
Carolyn, my best local friend
Frank, my pastor at St. Stephen's
Todd, my wise and playful buddy
My mother (sometimes)
Gene and Joan next door (sometimes)

Deirdre was devastated when her husband was killed several years ago. She characterized herself as "a very private person" and apologized for her reluctance to be interviewed, even though her pastor friend, Frank, recruited her for my study. I experienced Deirdre as very shy. Thus, I was surprised when she told me that except for her mother, her friends all knew whom she was dating at any given time, and whether there was sexual involvement or not. Believe it or not, this shy, private woman regularly took each of her friends into her confidence regarding her sexual vulnerability and current well-being.

Private and shy or not, I found Deirdre wise. She was not afraid to "aim high." Her friends were male and female, older and younger, similar and different; there was both depth and breadth in her support system. And she really invited them into her life! I formed the clear impression that Deirdre will cope with whatever comes and will not get hurt beyond her ability to handle it (as she put it) "with a little help from my friends."

The fifth task to pursue is to *learn to talk about your sexual self.*

I know long-married people who cannot discuss their sexual wants and needs, not even with their spouses. Their marriages suffer greatly because of it. One cannot afford to live without this skill.

The place to start talking is with your friends, at first one-on-one and then in a group. Unless you date neanderthals or nitwits, once you are truly free to verbalize who you are as a sexual being, who your friends are, and what they mean to you, and what you will and will not permit, you need have little fear about your sexual safety.

What to Avoid

First, *avoid putting your sex life on hold until you have a lover.* For one thing, as bleak as it may sound, you may never have a lover. If you are a heterosexual woman, be aware that from midlife on your options will diminish. This is because of the sexism in our culture (enabling men to marry women many years their junior) and because women live longer than men. If you are a heterosexual man, be aware that women increasingly refuse to court "down the ladder." For instance, one woman who earns a six-figure salary said, "I date only men who earn more than I." Her statement may be unfair or silly, but I heard her say it.

For another thing, if you wait until you have a lover to express your sexuality, your vulnerability may be far too great for you to maintain objectivity about the relationship. You will be projecting, a dangerous procedure at best.

Let me explain.

Second, *avoid projection.* When we project, we believe a person or object has our ideas, attitudes, or feelings. One delusionally assumes that "I have found my perfect mirror image. Here is somebody who thinks, speaks, feels, and acts just like me!" Projection may be useful for connecting—in fact, to some degree it is unavoidable in initial encounters—but it is not useful for sustaining a relationship. It never was. Projection is "an illusion of fusion." Such an illusion is a flight of fancy on gossamer wings—pleasant, but fleeting and unreal.

Third, *avoid courting inappropriate people.* Be free to explore a variety of relationships, but ask yourself: "Why do I want to have a second date with this person?" For one thing, if your first outing did not furnish sufficient data for you to answer the question, it is unlikely a second date will. If you cannot answer your question clearly and affirmatively, skip the second date.

For another thing, it is easier to say no to a second date than to a third. I know people who dated for months or even years someone they neither loved nor wanted—a cruelty to both parties, ending in deep hurt. Learn to say no to a second date.

A Crucial Question

What is the least for which you will settle?

A sexually whole single has incorporated her maleness (or his femaleness) into the self and no longer needs to seek it in another. Such a one, having become sexually self-supporting, will not be particularly role-oriented, power-oriented, or defensive. She or he will not be like the poor soul who lamented, "I'm really not a defensive person—unless I'm with somebody else or by myself." Sexually whole singles are defensiveless, about their sexuality as well as the rest of themselves.

When one is defensiveless, one can intelligently decide what one will settle for, where one will set one's minimum standard for a relationship.

Keeping in mind that all relationships have an implicitly sexual dimension, here is a model I have experimented with and rewritten many times. It has become my own—my personal "rule of thumb" in pursuing relationships that may, or may not, ever become explicitly sexual.

The Love Relationship

I love me. Here is what I mean: My need to do my own thing, and my right to be me, are immeasurably precious to me. The thoughts I think, the emotions I feel, the words I speak, and the actions I take are mine. They all are freely chosen by me, and for them I am totally responsible. Whether satisfying or not, they are my "thing"—my experiment in actualizing my own singlehood, my opportunity to learn from my own experience, my expression of my love for me.

But . . . I also love you. Here is what I mean: Your need to do your own thing, and your right to be you, are equally precious to me. The thoughts you think, the emotions you feel, the words you speak, and the actions you take are yours. They all are freely chosen by you, and for them I am in no way responsible. Whether satisfying or not, they are your "thing"—your experiment in actualizing your own singlehood, your opportunity to learn from your own experience, your expression of your love for you.

Now I am aware that behind any resentment I feel in our relationship is my demand that you change—my demand that you think and feel and speak and act the way I prescribe. I am also aware that this is both unfair and unsatisfying. It would be far better, in an attitude of love, to meet each other in the middle—to defensive*less*ly negotiate whatever might make for mutual need satisfaction, since I am aware, too, that the best interests of each one of us will best be served through careful attention to the best interests of both of us. So, to restore my own attitude of love for me and equally for you, and to express my sincere desire for mutuality, I here and now cancel all my demands. I reaffirm that you are not in this world to live up to my expectations, any more than I am in this world to live up to your expectations.

You are you, the you I love. I am I, the self I love. And if in being ourselves we find each other from time to time, it's beautiful. If not, it's sad . . . but it can't be helped; for such a finding-of-each-other can come only in that moment of love when, simultaneously, you and I each fully appreciate, and fully affirm, the other person as lovable *as is.* This can happen. It has happened before. I want it to happen again. I hope it will happen to us, and I willingly assume whatever responsibility is mine for its happening. I cherish that prospect.

But, even if it never happens, I am relaxed in the freedom of loving me, and loving you, as we are. For because I "know" in the innermost core of my being the truth that love is *the* attitude with which to perceive you, as well as me, I am indeed free—free to be me, and free to affirm your freedom to be you.

That is what I mean when I say: I love me. I love you.[14]

The above model is not engraved in stone, not to be idolized. Some find it too idealistic. By the same token, one can criticize the Great Commandment of the Judeo-Christian tradition: "You shall love the Lord your God with all your heart, and with all your soul, and with all your mind, and with all your strength," and *"your neighbor as your self,"* an ideal to which millions have aspired, although none has ever attained it fully. But if you prefer, build and embrace a model of your own.

Still, as a singling adult you must come to terms with the question "What is the least for which you will settle?" It is the big question about all your relationships—lover-to-lover, child-to-parent, or friend-to-friend.

11

Where to Find Help

At singles events the most common question that is asked is: Where can I go for help with my singling? This chapter attempts to respond.

The previous chapter stated that we are at the same time physical, intellectual, emotional, interpersonal (social), sexual, and spiritual beings. We may go to physicians for physical help, and to wise teachers or authors for intellectual help. But how about help with our other ways of being? Our feelings? interpersonal foibles? sexual hang-ups? Or our empty souls?

There are folks who can help. Some of them might not like the label, but let's call them "professional people helpers." Who are they, and how can the struggling singler find just the right one? Listen to Lou Ann's story.

> I figured that since I was the one who got me into this mess, it was up to me to get me out of it. After all, no one taught me how to screw up my life—I figured it out all by myself. No one taught me how to keep getting egg on my face, either—I set it up all by myself. So when we finally split up and Charlie, my ex, said, "You'd better get some help!" that was like waving a red flag in front of a bull. My philosophy was, God helps those who help themselves, thankyouverymuch.
>
> That was five years ago, and here I am in therapy now and in church too. So I suppose you want to know what happened. *(Pause)*

(INTERVIEWER: Yes, I do.)

Well, let's just say I grew up. Or I'm finally trying to grow up. I mean, it's a long story. If you really want to hear it . . .

(INTERVIEWER: I do.)

It was a long story. Lou Ann is only in her twenties, but it took her ninety minutes to bring me up to the present. She was unraveling and reweaving a lifelong pattern of basic mistrust. It began when, as a little girl, her father let her down terribly, again and again. Those memories had not healed. Sexually active from an early age, she had lived a life of promiscuity and shame. Now something had to happen before she could make a commitment to any important relationship. She was making a start. For openers, she had committed her life to God.

Most details of Lou Ann's life don't matter here. Many of us, unless we are very young, have long stories.

What got Lou Ann into therapy and church does matter.

After her brief marriage ended in divorce, several years of what she called "superficial fun and games" left Lou Ann very empty. Then two things happened almost simultaneously: Lou Ann found a man she desperately wanted, as a conquest, but was utterly unable to win despite her cleverest ploys (as she put it, "I'd met my match"); and a woman friend from work enticed Lou Ann into accompanying her to a weekend singles conference sponsored by a Presbyterian church. "There'll be lots of eligible men" was all Lou Ann needed to hear.

Lou Ann came away from the conference without a new lover but with two new resolves: to join the church's singles group and to try counseling with a woman therapist who spoke at the conference. I met her some weeks later.

Help for Your Singling: Counseling Help

The professional people-helping business can be a confusing morass. Since I am both a minister and a mental health professional, let me try to sort out the field, at the risk of offending some people.

First, a word about psychotherapy: Psychotherapy is not for everyone.

In certain circles it is the new religion, the "in" thing. A cocktail party conversation might go something like this:

"My therapist is Fritz Stiegelitz. He's the greatest. He makes me work *so-o-o* hard. I never know what the man's going to do next. He is definitely crazy, and I think I'm definitely in love with him."

"How long have you been going to him?"

"Nine years."

"Well, that's nice. I quit my male shrink when he raised his fee for the third time in three years. We weren't getting anyplace anyway. I did all the talking; he never said diddly squat. But now I'm with Samantha Samoyed. She's the greatest. She makes me work *so-o-o* hard."

"Well, that's nice."

Psychotherapy is not for everyone. Some people are not apt to benefit much and probably ought not to bother. Forrest is an example. He is a distinguished lawyer, an astute political scientist, great fun to be with, and an avid reader. During his wife's terminal illness he asked me for a reading list and devoured every book on the list, reflecting intelligently whenever we talked. He is a lifelong Episcopalian, and after his wife died he intensified his church involvements. The last I heard he was doing just fine—living alone, leading retreats, and meeting occasionally with his "spiritual director," a Roman Catholic theology professor who is a nun. To push psychotherapy at Forrest as a necessary singling activity would be absurd.

Second, a word about timing: It is foolish to "push the river." There is a timing to one's growth readiness. For instance, some of us, like Norma, are late bloomers. It is the way we are.

> It would have been lovely if I could have had my adolescence when I was an adolescent. That would have been the best time for it. But I was too tied up with trying to please everybody else but me; so I had no adolescence then. As I've thought about it, I tried to begin my adolescence during my senior year in high school. But it scared

> me, so I squelched it. I picked it up again in college, but then shut it down once I met my fiancé. I married as soon as I graduated from college, so I ignored my need for an adolescence right on through the birth of my two children—after all, I always had to behave in an exemplary fashion for their sake, didn't I?
>
> Well, my adolescence erupted like a volcano several years later, in grad school. Somehow, as I worked on my master's degree while my husband built his career, and with my kids both in school, I was able to permit myself the developmental task I should have tackled as a teenager. I'm not proud of this, mind you; but at thirty I got myself into a torrid affair with a man nearly ten years younger.

When Norma sought professional counseling, it was to help her decide whether to divorce and how to complete her belated adolescence. She was ready to use help wisely.

When grief is not going well, when memories are not healing, when lonesomeness is overwhelming, when one wants to make changes but fights against it, time with a helper can be a rewarding investment.

One's individual need system must inform timing; no two people have the same needs. However, one's singling time is often an ideal time to concentrate on personal and spiritual growth issues. Because marriages and other primary relationships consume energy and time, the acquisition of new social skills, intellectual improvement, spiritual deepening, and other growth tasks are usually easier to pursue while single. If it feels like the right time, seek help now. Later may be too late.

Short-term Help Is Available

Many singlers avoid seeking help because they believe that once they start they must continue for years and years.

Some therapists do prefer (or insist on) steady, long-term relationships with their clients. This is perfectly legitimate, and some people surely need it. Still, many helpers do accept short-term counselees.

Short-term helpers often use a more action-oriented approach than psychoanalysts or other long-term therapists. Typically, at the close of the initial interview they will ask for a start-up agreement (for example, six weekly meetings to get to know one another). After that, they will review and negotiate the helper-helpee "contract" as needed. By all means, ask a potential helper how she or he works before your second appointment.

Choosing a Helper

First, when it comes to the art of people-helping *a helper's labels do not matter much.* (Basic credentials do matter—see what follows.) The marketplace offers a variety of helpers with a seemingly endless array of approaches. When one looks at results, however, it is quite impossible to tell the difference between good psychoanalysis, good psychotherapy, and good counseling; or between a counselee, a client, and a therapy patient.

The "cast of characters" who do professional counseling includes:

- The psychiatrist, who is always a physician but not necessarily trained in psychoanalysis or even in counseling (most psychiatrists *are* experts at psychopharmacology);
- The psychoanalyst, who may or may not be a medical doctor but who has had extensive training in (Freudian) psychoanalysis;
- The Jungian, Adlerian, Sullivanian, or other analyst, physician or "lay," who has been schooled in the approaches of Jung, Adler, Sullivan, or others;
- The psychologist, who usually has a Ph.D. or Ed.D. degree and often a specialty (clinical, child, industrial, for example);
- The pastoral counselor, usually an ordained clergyperson with an advanced degree in counseling plus clinical training[1] and ecclesiastical endorsement to practice therapy as a ministerial specialty;[2]
- The spiritual director, who works under the auspices of a church organization or religious order (spiritual directors

are commonest within the Roman Catholic and Episcopal or Anglican traditions);

- The minister, priest, or rabbi who is a parish clergyperson. Nowadays, many clergy are good counselors; seminaries and those who ordain clergy insist on training in counseling. If you have a pastor, begin there. Your pastor will discuss his or her limits with you and refer you to additional help if advisable. If you trust your pastor, you can trust the helper to whom you are referred;
- The LCSW (Licensed Clinical Social Worker), who has a master's degree in social work (MSW) plus clinical training;
- The MFCC (Marriage, Family, and Child Counselor) who has at least a master's degree in counseling plus clinical training;
- Someone with one or more of the above "tickets" who prefers to use another title, such as Gestalt Therapist, Transactional Analyst, Reality Therapist, Hypnotherapist;

and last, and definitely least:

X someone with *none* of the above "tickets," who manages to get around state licensure laws by using a clever label or gimmick in order to sound like a legitimate therapist.

Confused? Bored? Found out more than you wanted to know? What you need to remember is that when it comes to the practical side of people-helping, *a helper's labels do not matter much* as long as the person is licensed, certified, or endorsed to practice. If you choose one of the above, take the trouble to check out your choice. What is his or her training? Under whose licensure or auspices does the person practice? In what professional organizations is he or she active?[3] How long has the person been in practice? If you have inadvertently stumbled onto a "type X" from the menu above, you'll be glad you figured it out before you wasted time and money needlessly.

Second, *a helper's views and values do matter.* What views does this person hold? What constitutes a "problem" that warrants treatment? By what method does she or he work? Also, how does this helper regard singlehood? That matters. You have a right to know. Ask. If what you hear is unclear or at odds with what you want, look elsewhere.

Third, don't use the Yellow Pages. *Seek a helper recommended by a trusted referral agent* or satisfied customer, and then interview the helper by telephone before you go. Good referral agents include clergy, physicians, and public health or community service workers. A telephone conversation with the recommended helper may be all you need to decide whether that particular helper is the one for you, or you may decide to go for an initial face-to-face interview. Remember, you needn't go back for a second interview if not satisfied. You are the consumer: Shop. Professional people helpers are human, and none of them connects with everybody. You need somebody you can open up to. (*Note:* If you "strike out" again and again, either you really do have a serious problem or you are using very poor referral resources!)

Fourth, *if you are a woman, a woman therapist may be preferable.* Of course, a skilled male therapist is preferable to an unskilled female one. But all things being equal (or unequal, given the sexism in our culture), a woman often profits most from a helper most likely to understand a woman's particular singling needs and the challenges she faces on her journey.

If you are a man, your main concern may be finding someone to help you become an androgynous single whose feminine side is in balance with his masculine side.[4] A skilled helper of either sex should be able to help.

Fifth, *a good helper is a good referral counselor.* She or he has a network of trusted colleagues and will not hesitate to refer you to another person or to a different kind of help, if it makes sense. Possible referrals may be for spiritual guidance, group therapy, family therapy for you and your children, career counseling, assertiveness training, sex therapy, or counseling with a helper of the other sex to work on a specific issue. No one helper can "do it all."

Sixth, *expensive does not necessarily mean better.* To most singles money is precious. There is no sense in wasting any. In the present context, four money issues are worth considering:

1. Psychiatrists usually charge the highest fees, but few sin-

gling adults need one. Psychiatrists are first of all physicians. They do lots of inpatient care in general and psychiatric hospitals; they must be skilled diagnosticians and prescribe medicines (psychotropic drugs) when nothing else will do; and an hour (usually fifty minutes) of their time is valuable. If your nonmedical therapist wants you to see a psychiatrist for a diagnostic consultation or prescription, do not hesitate to go. But don't assume you must seek a psychiatrist to find good therapy. Some psychiatrists are excellent interviewers (psychotherapists). Others are not.

Note: Physicians routinely refer their patients to other physicians. If you ask your doctor for a therapy referral, you will likely be sent to a psychiatrist.

2. Nonmedical helpers include clergy, psychologists, pastoral counselors, clinical social workers, and marriage and family therapists. (Remember: A therapist's labels do not matter much.) Psychotherapeutic interviewing is what these people do. Again, you will want a trained, accredited person, but licensure is no guarantee of skill. Some are highly skilled, others are not; there is no direct correlation between credentials and expertise.

3. Fees vary widely in different settings and locales, from the community mental health center or pastoral counseling center with a sliding fee scale (based on ability to pay) to the private practitioner.

A rule of thumb is: Usually, psychologists charge less than psychiatrists but more than the other helpers. Clergy or spiritual directors often negotiate fees idiosyncratically; for example, a contribution to their church or school may be agreed on in lieu of a fee. Always inquire about fees before you start. If it matters, ask whether the fee is negotiable or not, and whether insurance is welcomed.

If you have health insurance, the odds are that licensed helpers are covered. Use your insurance! However, different policies cover different kinds of helpers. Check with your carrier ahead of time to understand your coverage and how to use it. Most helpers expect you to pay as you go (which is only fair), but they will help you collect reimbursements.

4. If your health insurance is with an "HMO" (health mainte-

nance organization), check to see what services it offers. Many HMOs are attuned to "growth therapy," have excellent counselors, and offer either individual or group programs. If, however, your particular HMO does not offer what you need as a singling person, do not let that keep you from seeking help elsewhere.

Help for Your Singling: Spiritual Help

Psychotherapy and spiritual direction—to coin a term, "theotherapy"—need not be at odds. They can go hand in hand, simply approaching life from different perspectives. Many psychotherapists are spiritually sophisticated, and many spiritual guides are psychologically sophisticated. Ideally, look for a helper who has both kinds of training and embodies the approach you prefer.[5]

Most people will do anything to avoid being pegged as pious, and singles feel that way more than most people. But there comes a time when the pursuit of spiritual growth, by whatever name, is the singler's task—a time when nothing else will do.

When the urge toward spiritual development comes, some call it the lure of a supreme being: God. But by whatever name, when the Spirit of Life beckons, when a longing for rebirth comes, one is wise to respond.

Let me suggest how the call might come and how one might answer by sharing with you the story of Daniel.

> Reared in a strict Christian home, Daniel bent to peer pressure in the tenth grade and dropped out of church, except for an occasional appearance to keep his parents off his back. Rock-and-roll music became his passion. A gifted drummer, he earned enough money to buy a car and attend college.
>
> In college he married Sherry, a singer as devoted to rock music as he. They literally made music together. They also made two children, and both Daniel and Sherry became public school teachers.
>
> No one was prepared for the doctor's ominous words: "I'm sorry, but Sherry has leukemia, the fast-acting kind."

> Daniel quickly led his family in the search for a church. They found one, joined it, and became the objects of much care and prayer. Then, barely a year after the diagnosis, Sherry died. Now a twenty-eight-year-old widower with two sons to raise, a tearful Daniel asked his minister, "What is the meaning of all this?"

Let's look at what Daniel learned and how he learned it.

What Spirituality Is

Spirituality is neither piety nor religiosity. Piety and religiosity refer to things one does, often in a compartmentalized way, time, and place. Spirituality is not a compartment of life at all, but the deepest dimension of all of life.

To describe the path of spiritual growth feels presumptuous, especially since it has been beautifully depicted by others. For example, buy a paperback copy of Scott Peck's *The Road Less Traveled* and read it (see the reading list).

To describe a spiritual person feels less presumptuous. I know Daniel. I can describe him as he is now. I did not know the Daniel whose Sherry contracted cancer years ago, but from hearing his story I gather he is very different now.

The most important concept in Daniel's life these days is the idea of connectedness—connectedness to his own being, to his personal history, to other people, and to the source of his being. He says he doesn't try to prioritize these forms of connectedness. For Daniel, they all fit together or else none of them is real.

So, one characteristic of spirituality is connectedness—I would say, with all that is.

There are other characteristics.[6] Here are Daniel's:

- Formerly a man who wanted what he wanted when he wanted it, Daniel now has patience with himself, others, and life. As a human pregnancy takes nine months, all growth takes its time. A spiritual person is in tune with the flow of life, tolerant of its natural processes, and able to wait for gratification.

- Daniel frequently expresses awe at the fragile beauty of life. He says, "I never knew what Sherry and I had until we lost it." To be reverent, even awestruck, at life all around us, and aware of its temporariness, is to care for it lovingly. Spiritual people do this.
- Daniel is an openly grateful man. This is clearly connec ted with awe, but it goes beyond it. Because thanksgiving presumes a giver, expressing gratefulness puts one squarely in contact with the Giver. Daniel calls the Giver "God."
- Daniel has a remarkable sense of perspective, the ability to distance oneself from the moment. People with perspective keep their wits about them, and have a sense of distance from everyday things. This helps them view both the new and the old with appropriate objectivity. Another word for perspective might be equilibrium.
- Along the way, Daniel developed a considerable capacity for contemplation. He learned to quit rushing life. He learned how to contemplate nature, himself, other people, and God. Contemplation, while a close relative of prayer (and, in some systems of religious practice, the highest form of prayer), simply means "looking at." Contemplation comes in solitude, silence, and standstill. Contemplation is greatly helped by patience, perspective, and reverence (the above characteristics are all interrelated).
- Daniel knows how to rework painful experiences and losses. This became evident recently when his love affair with Belinda, whom he secretly hoped to marry, fizzled. Having grieved Sherry's loss wisely and completely, he knows how to grieve lesser losses and heal his memory.
- He knows how to forgive, and does. The peril of not forgiving is that the unforgiving person cannot experience forgiveness. (Jesus said that.) Belinda, the never-married woman who cut and ran when the relationship got serious, said she felt intimidated by the idea of becoming stepmother to Daniel's two sons. Daniel felt no need to judge her. In fact, he said, "If you were a widow with two sons and I had no children, I'd feel threatened too."

- He has simplified his everyday life. Daniel and his sons now live an uncluttered life. Daniel sold the "dream house" he and Sherry bought. In its place he purchased a condominium whose maintenance is insured. Says Daniel, "Some things, while good, are simply not worth our precious time now, if they ever were. What time I have I want to invest in service to my boys and others."
- Daniel has become a lifelong learner. Currently he is learning about metamorphosis, or transformation. Like the legendary phoenix, he rose from the ashes of his wife's death to life in a new form, and he got excited about the possibilities of deaths and new births. No one is perfect, but Daniel's skill at transformation is impressive. Even his most skeptical friends are amazed at the new Daniel.

Starting in a Congregation

The way to start is by finding a house of worship.

Churches and synagogues are seeking out never married and formerly married people as never before. When Sherry died, Daniel was surprised by the number of church people who shared their stories with him—stories of death, of divorce, or of a man rearing his daughter alone after his wife ran away soon after their baby was born. Daniel's minister says one third of that particular congregation's members are unmarried adults.

But, unfortunately, Daniel's congregation has few programs aimed specifically at singling persons. Because a nearby congregation specializes in singles ministry along ecumenical (interfaith) lines, Daniel began to go there each Sunday evening. (That's where he met Belinda.)

Daniel found benefits that are not just social. Among those benefits is a fixed reference point for one's life, a still place in an otherwise moving existence. Another benefit is a ready-made family, a place to belong. A third is that participating in congregational affairs helps a person feel like a certified adult making a contribution to society.

Daniel began to see that his music, and then his marriage, had represented pseudo religions for him. He remembered asking Sherry to marry him with the words "I adore you," and he says he continued to worship her throughout their years together. He now needed a fresh faith.

Then, as Daniel met regularly with other singling seekers, some talked about their therapists or spiritual directors. He consulted his pastor, who gave him the names of some of each and told him to shop. He now admits he asked more out of curiosity than from genuine interest: "I didn't even know what these people did." He knows now. He also met with his pastor periodically to share his progress. The pastor always congratulated him and cheered him on.

A person never becomes mature in isolation. Daniel found that being a lone ranger would not do. He began to share himself with others, something he'd never done before, and he experienced a kind of love he calls "agape . . . which I never knew existed."

Daniel says it helped to attend several church-sponsored retreats for singles: "Several close friendships began on those retreats."

"Looking back on it, it all seems kind of simple now," Daniel says. "Whenever someone I respected suggested something to read, I read it. When an event looked appealing, I went. When someone suggested I attend a national conference for singles, I took a week's vacation and went. It was the greatest week of my year."

Daniel learned the easy way.

Direction from a Hospital Chaplain

Elfriede learned the hard way. When her husband left her for a younger woman, she was devastated. Months turned into years in which she moped and nursed her bitterness. "What am I to do, a middle-aged woman with no skills or prospects?" she whined. In despair one midwinter night, she swallowed a bottle of sleeping pills.

Fortunately, her suicide attempt took place in the home of her sister and brother-in-law. When they returned from a dinner party and found her, they called an ambulance.

At the county hospital the next day, Chaplain Markham called on Elfriede:

CHAPLAIN: Elfriede.
ELFRIEDE: That's me . . .
CHAPLAIN: What brings you to the hospital?
ELFRIEDE: I tried to kill myself. *(Pause)* I wish I'd succeeded.
CHAPLAIN: A cry for help.
ELFRIEDE: A cry for help? What do you mean?
CHAPLAIN: When a person tries to kill herself and doesn't succeed, I see it as a cry for help.
ELFRIEDE: *(Long pause)* No one can help.
CHAPLAIN: Oh?
ELFRIEDE: I have nothing to live for.
CHAPLAIN: Tell me more.
ELFRIEDE: *(Tells her story about her husband's infidelity)*
CHAPLAIN: Why do you want to stay married to a guy like that?
ELFRIEDE: Oh, he divorced me and married her.
CHAPLAIN: That's what he did, but you seem to be still married to him.
ELFRIEDE: How can you tell that?
CHAPLAIN: You haven't let go of him. *(Silence . . . then quietly)* Maybe it's time to let what is dead be dead, so Elfriede can live.
ELFRIEDE: How do I do that?
CHAPLAIN: On your chart it says you are Lutheran.
ELFRIEDE: Yes. All my life.
CHAPLAIN: There has to be a Good Friday before there can be an Easter.
ELFRIEDE: *(Long pause)* Jesus had to die first.
CHAPLAIN: First the crucifixion, then the resurrection.
ELFRIEDE: I'm beginning to see what you mean. My marriage has to die before I can have a new life.

Elfriede stayed in the hospital for one week. Chaplain Markham saw her twice each day. Reborn, Elfriede began to live. The day after she left the hospital was a Sunday. She woke up early, put on her best clothes, and went to church.

During the following months, Elfriede rarely missed church. She took her pastor's advice and began to see a therapist.

Today she is anything but suicidal. One evening every week she answers the hot line at a nearby suicide prevention center. She also chairs the singles ministry in her church.

Psychotherapy and Spiritual Direction

Theology is the oldest of the "spirit sciences." Psychology is the youngest. For centuries priests, rabbis, pastors, or shamans did whatever healing, sustaining, reconciling, and guiding got done. Mental-emotional-spiritual health were viewed as one and the same (along with physical health, for that matter). Then came the disciplinary organization of knowledge and the age of specialization.

Now we have recovered the knowledge that a person is indeed an organic whole, and that everything about her or him affects everything else about her or him.[7] Still, today, ministers and mental health professionals must share the honors as growth facilitators, and psychotherapy substitutes for religion in many lives. That which is new, allegedly scientific, and expensive is seen as superior to that which is ancient, inherently mysterious, and a gift of grace.

But let me be more practical and concrete.

First, if you come from a religious background, now is the ideal time to renew this dimension. You might find that while you were changing and growing, your church or synagogue changed and grew too. At least, start there. If you don't find what you need, then look for it elsewhere.

Second, as in Daniel's case, your church or synagogue may be the best place, and your pastor the best person, to help you find what you need—a substitute family, a singles fellowship, a growth group, or a suitable therapist. Chances are, your pastor can help you determine what you need and see to it that you get to an appropriate helper to meet your need. Often clergy are the best referral counselors in the community.

Third, to reinforce a point, psychotherapy and spiritual direction are not mutually exclusive. (If your religion sees them that way, find another church!) Singling adults grow better, and faster, if they anchor themselves to a faith system and then use psychotherapy as an adjunct to it, not as a substitute for it.

Finally, "the ultimate goal of life remains the spiritual growth of the individual, the solitary journey to peaks that can be climbed only alone."[8] Each of us must climb his or her peak in a unique way. Psychotherapy may help. So may spiritual direction, whether by participation in the general life of a congregation, the wise counsel of a minister, priest, or rabbi, or involvement in a ministry specifically for singles. None of these possibilities should be overlooked.

Today Is the Day

Speaking from my own tradition, the Bible says, "Behold, now is the accepted time; behold, now is the day of salvation" (2 Cor. 6:2, KJV).

So start now. If you are thirty and your spouse just left you for a twenty-year-old, start now. If you are eighty and want eighty-one to be better, start now. It's the only place you can begin.

As I write this I realize I am fifty and still don't know who or what I want to be when I grow up. But I am determined to keep growing up. I hope to die growing up. And for me, growing up means growing up spiritually. "The Spirit . . . produces in human life fruits such as these: love, joy, peace, patience, kindness, generosity, fidelity, tolerance and self-control—and no law exists against any of them." (Gal. 5:22–23, PHILLIPS).

12

Lifestyle Issues

Three additional mine fields warrant flagging. They do not apply to all singling adults (the very rich and the very old may skip this chapter) but plenty of single journeys have been stalled, and hearts have been broken, because of parental pressure, financial distress, or the inability to live alone. Do not let these forces undermine you.

You and Your Non-Single Parents

For insight into how parental pressure can hold back the singling process, we might look at the different experiences of Madeline, Max, Anthony, and Esther. Let's hear Madeline's story first:

> Divorce was the hardest thing I had ever done, but now I think I'm going through something harder. I'm talking about my parents. That's where I really need help. I may have been able to get rid of Aaron when I found out he was cheating on me, but how can I get rid of my parents?
>
> Don't misunderstand me; my folks are wonderful and mean well. But just when I need to become single they want to be my mommy and daddy again. I get called every day at home and often at work too. . . . Talk about embarrassing. . . . My father calls the office and he goes, "This is Madeline's father. Can I say hello to my little girl?" to the *receptionist!* She's the biggest gossip in the whole build-

> ing, and jealous of my position in the company. I could've died.
>
> Like I said, they mean well. But they act as if I never left home, never got married, never had their granddaughter. They want me over for dinner as often as possible, but then when I go they grill me about every aspect of my life. And I can't win. First they criticize how I handle the baby. Then Mother gets on me about my weight while she's feeding me mashed potatoes and banana cream pie. Then they ask who I'm seeing these days, and when I tell them they tell me I ought to date a better class of "nice young men." *(Pause . . . sigh)* Just last night Mother had the nerve to ask if I was brushing my teeth! She insists they used to be whiter.

Madeline's parents married forty years ago. She was their youngest child and only daughter. Well-to-do and conservative, they were accustomed to "all things done decently and in order," as Madeline's father put it. Openly, they blamed Aaron for the divorce, but subtly they blamed Madeline for marrying Aaron over their objection that he wasn't good enough. Probably they blamed themselves for failing to be perfect parents, too. Now they felt responsible for their daughter's welfare and wanted to correct their "mistakes." Parents recapitulate their motherly/fatherly roles when their adult children become single.

Max, a fifty-eight-year-old widower, enthusiastically volunteered for a year's service in a Third World country. An early retiree with thirty years' experience as a civil engineer, ample money, and time on his hands, he glowed as he said, "I have a new lease on life, a chance to make a difference in this world. I'm gonna build a dam!" How crushed Max felt when forced to cancel his plans after his mother threatened to kill herself if he did such a silly thing.

Anthony was in the throes of a painful separation after years of marital therapy and careful consideration. He clearly wanted a divorce, but his parents pushed him mercilessly to reconcile with his estranged wife, saying, "We don't care what you think is in your best interest. After all we've done for you, you owe us this much. No one divorces in this family." They vowed to disinherit him if he insisted on divorcing.

A mother hounded her newly widowed daughter, Esther, to begin dating and tried to "fix her up" with eligible men, instead of encouraging her to take time to grieve and become comfortably single. An exasperated Esther asked, "How can I be a loving, faithful daughter without compromising my integrity as a free person? I'm forty years old! The last thing I need is Golda the Matchmaker for a mother."

Esther's question was a good one. How does one relate to one's parents responsibly without compromising the singling process? How does one act lovingly toward parents or other family members while also living one's own life experiment, when the experiment threatens them because they are non-singles? Here are five ideas that may help.

First, as a singling adult *it is legitimate, and may be necessary, to "divorce" one's parents.* This may seem harsh, but many singles, after a marriage ends, or the son or daughter simply moves from the family home to a different location, find they must follow through with another kind of clean-cut separation, this time from their childhood ties to mother, father, siblings, or grandparents. All relationships end in separations, always. *Singling involves mastering the art of separating.*

For those with a religious background I offer a rationale from the Christian tradition. Jesus was a single man. He began singling at age twelve and was wholly single when at age thirty he left his family, forever. I assume a biblical principle relevant to divorcing one's family from one of his more peculiar sayings:

> Do not think that I have come to bring peace on earth; I have not come to bring peace, but a sword. For I have come to set a son against his father, and a daughter against her mother, and a daughter-in-law against her mother-in-law; and one's foes will be those of one's own household. Whoever loves father or mother more than me is not worthy of me; and whoever loves son or daughter more than me is not worthy of me; and those who do not take their own cross and follow me are not worthy of me. Those who find their life will lose it, and those who lose their life for my sake will find it.[1]

Jesus is not speaking out against the family, but he may be reminding his followers that he did not come to earth to guarantee them comfort and peace and a pleasant life. Jesus tells us that often, if you are faithful to yourself and to your mission in life, you will pay a price.

You may need to choose between living the truth and keeping the peace. You may reap trouble and argument even in your own family if you break from their tradition. "Image" and a corporate identity are important to some families. "What will our relatives think?" "What will the neighbors say?" "How can I show my face at the church or the club?" "How can you do this to us?" Families want smooth sailing and will do almost anything, including outright lying, to have it! So even where you most dearly long for acceptance, you may be forced to choose between a "fake peace," purchased at the price of faithfulness to yourself, and a commitment that leads to a solitary journey into the unknown.

The point is worth emphasizing. Many devoutly religious people who idolize marriage and the family view singling with condescension and concern or condemnation. They regard marriage and childbearing as the will of God for everyone. Whoever chooses to move toward singlehood may be seen as "stepping right out of the will of God," as one mother said to her daughter. I have seen singling alienate many people from their parents. In other words, the "divorce" may not be a friendly one.

Second, *embrace the truth that you are now becoming more "grown up" than your parents.* Do it humbly, simply. Recognize that your maturation is not happening because of any virtue of your own, but it is happening. As today's singling adult you have all kinds of helps and advantages your parents never had. Don't expect them to understand, let alone accept, your new awareness or identity or lifestyle. They may not want to.

Third, *stop acting like your parents' child;* and fourth, *don't expect your parents to act like your friends.* Expect them to act like your parents.

When Erica walked out on her abusive husband, she fled to her parents' home. Six months later she decided it was important to live alone. This time she had to walk out on her abusive parents. In Erica's words:

> When you're in as much pain as I was, it's so easy to go to the one place where you know it's safe. It was safe, all right—the way a prison is safe. As soon as I wanted to live my own life, it was as if I was back in high school. "Where are you going?" "With whom?" "Dressed like that?" I kid you not, my mother threw out half of my wardrobe—all my jeans and most of my casual clothes. She wants me in silk dresses all the time! And a girdle!

If you want your parents to treat you like an adult you must behave like one, whether they like it or not. Running to "Mommy" or "Daddy" for a financial bailout, free child care, and home-cooked dinners may seem innocent enough, but such actions may signal your parents that you really are still their boy or girl.

Fifth and most important of all, *have mercy on your parents.* The more single you become, the more you will "see" what your parents do not need to see; the more you will hear what your parents do not need to hear; the more you will understand what your parents do not need to understand; and the more you will experience what your parents do not need to know about.

So . . . what to do?

There's no easy formula. But let your parents ask the questions. Don't lie, but minimize the information you volunteer. If you don't initiate information, they won't ask about it the next time you talk. If, on the other hand, you offer, "I really need to get to the dentist for my annual checkup before my teeth rot out of my head, but I just can't find time," you can bet your checkup will get put on your parents' "To Do" list. And they'll expect you to report whether your dentist found any cavities.

Despite the difficulty, many have managed the separation successfully. Ida is a single clergywoman. She is not opposed to marrying (she likes officiating at weddings) but has never married. The only child of alcoholic parents who are not at all religious, Ida began divorcing her family when she "rebelled" into the church during high school. Her parents helped Ida through college, hoping she would find a husband there, but they refused to support her in any way when she enrolled in a theological seminary. It hurt when they attended neither her seminary graduation nor her ordination to the priesthood. But she did not allow her parents' nonsupport to dissuade her from her goal.

Wise beyond her years, Ida enjoys a successful ministry and a very full singlehood. But let her speak for herself. The following excerpt is from her sermon at a singles conference where she was worship leader:

> People sometimes ask, "Why aren't you married yet?" and I can only say, "Because it has never been my time." Or they will ask, "Have you been single all your life?" My favorite rejoinder to that one is "Not yet." Others bait my maternal instincts by reminding me I'd better hurry up before I get too old to bear children. They're never sure whether I'm serious when I remind them that Sarah, the Old Testament matriarch, was pushing ninety when she and Abraham got pregnant.
>
> The Old Testament promises that "they that wait upon the Lord shall renew their strength." It does not say "loiter," but it does say "wait." I have. And I am. I hold to the firm hope that if I do just that, the salvation that is happening to me now as a single woman will come to full fruition exactly when, and how, God has in mind. I do not know what that means. But whatever else it means, it means I have plenty of time.[2]

Incidentally, it is rumored that Ida's parents brag constantly about their daughter's accomplishments (behind her back, of course). They probably still wish she wasn't ordained, and they might like it if she got married and pregnant—but apparently no one would ever know it to hear them crowing about their daughter the priest.

Singling and Money

Men and women may have different kinds of financial pressures, especially when children are involved, but financial problems can really put the squeeze on the singling process. Hear Polly's story:

> Money. Now there's a topic. You sure you really want me to talk about money? OK—how much are you paying me for this interview? *(Laughs)* Just kidding.
>
> Seriously, when it comes to money I'm a mess. I didn't used to be, but I swear things not only got worse when Ted and I split up, it keeps on getting worse. With one of my kids in child care and the other in preschool, my car falling apart, my rent raised twice in the past year, and Ted always late with the child support, it's touch and go whether we're going to eat or the kids are going to get to the doctor. I thought of the doctor because both kids are due for check-ups right now.
>
> Sometimes I turn down a date . . . simply because I can't afford a sitter or decent clothes . . . and I'm too embarrassed to just come right out and say that.

Joshua shared his story at a workshop:

> Maybe I care about money too much. But being single is just damned expensive. I bought some new clothes and a new car after my divorce, to cheer me up I guess. And I rented a nice apartment and furnished it, thinking I'd entertain some—after all, she got the house, why should I live in a dump? But here's the point. I make a good income, yet I've never been so broke in my life, and with very little to show for it. *(Pause)* You know, I hate credit cards with a passion. I'd like to cut them all in little pieces. But I've got a bunch of 'em like everybody else, and right now every one of 'em is loaded to the max.

Polly and Joshua may be atypical. Some singling people have more money, and better control of it, than they did when they were non-single. But the singling road can be financially rocky. It is difficult for one person to thrive on the income one person can earn.

To add to the problem some individuals, when they were non-single, relied on somebody else as their money manager and now that person is gone. Other singlers have simply never developed money management skills.

> Margot felt elated when she received her divorce settlement—the house, the furnishings, the newer of the two cars, adequate child support, and a generous spousal maintenance allowance. Her attorney, obviously pleased, said, "I've seen a lot of these cases and you really got the long end of the stick." One year later Margot asked the same lawyer to help assess her current financial condition. The lawyer advised her to file for bankruptcy.

There is no magic about money. Money is simply a medium of exchange. There's nothing moral or immoral about it. For the singling adult, however, money management skills are a "must," for several reasons.

First, when one has less to spend and only oneself to rely on, mistakes are relatively more costly.

Second, many a would-be single stays non-single, becoming a "kept" woman or man or marrying an inappropriate person, because of financial fright or ignorance.

Third, the government exacts a big tax bite from singles. This is unfair, but until singles band together as a bloc and lobby for reforms, the picture is unlikely to change. Lawmakers are mostly non-singles trying to please non-single constituents.

Fourth, home ownership is usually a taxpayer's biggest tax break as well as a hedge against inflation and a forced savings program. Many singles cannot afford to buy homes. Those who valiantly try to save a down payment while having to subsist on a single income often become discouraged and give up.

Fifth, singling itself can cost money. For example, choosing to live alone for its learning or healing value can worsen a singling person's financial struggles. So can striving for a better life by going back to school, joining a singles organization, or seeking counseling. Insufficient money affects one's spirits, self-esteem, outlook on life, and physical health.

I lay no claim to money-management expertise. The following ideas are from singling adults themselves. Some are money managers who make their living that way; most are folks like you who learned about money the hard way.

Earn as much money as possible. If you want a nest egg for tomorrow, your income must exceed your expenses today. You may scoff, but millions of your peers do not see the logic of this argument. If you are doing your best on your job, are your employers doing their best by you? Are you coasting along, afraid to present your employers with your needs and rights and their responsibility? Some people jeopardize their personal welfare under the guise of protecting their employers! "I wouldn't want to hurt my boss's feelings." "I know they're doing the best they can." "They have good fringe benefits."

As a singling adult, *you must take responsibility for your own financial well-being or no one will.* If this means adding on a part-time job or seeking an employer who will pay more, so be it. If it means seeking additional training, do it. Evening or weekend classes have the additional benefit of helping you meet people with similar interests; often they turn out to be helpful social or professional contacts.

If it means getting career counseling to formulate a "game plan" leading to a better-paying job, do it.[3] Even if you like your job, as a single you may not be able to afford the next ten years as a salesclerk, secretary, schoolteacher, or farm worker.

Continuing as an underemployed or underpaid "nice guy" or "sweet gal" won't make it. It won't even give you the self-respect you need in order to feel worthy of others' respect, let alone the power of a financially self-supporting single.

Pay yourself first. Elsie voiced this idea of paying yourself first at a singles retreat sponsored by a group of churches. The moment she suggested it another woman objected: "I was taught that as a Christian I am to give the 'firstfruits' of my labors to God." Without a moment's hesitation Elsie responded.

> OK, then; pay yourself second. But can you honestly say that because you love yourself just as you love God and just as God loves you, you are as good a steward toward yourself as you are toward God?
>
> I couldn't. I spent forty years putting not just God's needs ahead of mine; I put everybody's needs ahead of

> mine. I even divorced on my husband's terms, using his lawyer. Because I wanted out of the marriage, I left with nothing but the clothes on my back after twenty years of doing half the work. I don't want to rob God of a single penny, and maybe I'm trying to make up for lost time. But even if that's so, I don't care. It's time Elsie took care of Elsie. *(The group applauded.)*

If you do not take a specific amount out of each paycheck for savings, you probably will not save at all. Many assume that savings will come from the surplus that remains after all other needs are met. The trouble is, there is seldom any surplus.

Somehow our needs expand to meet our income, no matter how much we earn. Thus the admonition: Pay yourself first. Make the amount you set aside for savings realistic, not so big that it kills you, but not so tiny that it doesn't hurt at all. The experts say regularity is the key; consistency is more important than the amount. One authority calls this a "positive addiction"—a habit that will do you good.

Where should you save? Volumes are written on the topic. A bit of reading can increase your knowledgeability not only about savings but also about budgeting and other money matters.[4] Two rules of thumb to remember: The older one is, the less risk one can afford (the young can recoup losses more easily); and, at any age, never invest in anything that will disturb your sleep.

Beware of debt. Singling people are prone to fiscal overextension. Advertising's power is pervasive, and singling time is one of extraordinary susceptibility. The appeals are cleverly conceived to play to our hungers for comfort, love, status, and happiness.

You may also be vulnerable to requests for donations. If you cannot afford a cash contribution "up front," resist, even though the cause may be noble and legitimate.

Theresa, a partner in an architectural firm, was already attuned to feminism and egalitarianism when she began singling. With her interest in women's rights, she received mailings from numerous women's organizations requesting contributions for worthwhile causes (pledges and credit cards gladly accepted). Before long she "owed" inordinate amounts of money. She was forced to cancel some of her pledges, a painful experience. Like many Americans, Theresa's earning skills were better than her money management skills.

If we want to stay financially solvent, say the experts, only two purchases justify credit: a residence and an automobile. All other items should be purchased with cash or checks. This takes courage and effort, but it can be done if one sets aside a portion of each month's income toward the purchase of business clothing, an appliance, a vacation trip, and other "big ticket" items.

Both financial advisers and psychologists issue one special warning worth underscoring for singles: *Be particularly cautious in buying an automobile.* Automobiles are often used, in our culture, to satisfy psychological hungers—for status, or to appeal to the opposite sex, for example. I know a singling man who purchased a thirty-five-thousand-dollar sports car, which effectively kept him broke for years. A carefully selected used car is often the best investment on a limited budget, but have it checked by a trustworthy mechanic before buying. If buying a residence is impossible or years away, an auto may be the biggest purchase you make. Do it wisely. Don't be "car poor."

The biggest boost to both savings and debt-free living is the simple avoidance of credit-card purchases. Card interest rates are high. One singling man said as he took a scissors to his stack of credit cards, "I may never be rich, but I needn't be dumb either." (He kept one lone card for check-writing identification.)

Consider living without an automobile. As radical as this idea may seem, some of the most creative singles I know have made it work. Billie Jean was one. She bought a condominium within walking distance of the school where she taught. The differential between owning an automobile and being car-free made home ownership possible. When she really needed a car, she rented one. It took sacrifice, but it paid off. It helped that Billie Jean lived in a city with good public transportation, but she planned it that way.

Car-free living may be impractical for you, but don't rule it out hastily. Thousands of dollars per year can be freed for savings, better housing, travel, or education. One can use taxicabs or rental cars prudently and still come out way ahead.

As I drafted this chapter on a rainy day, an old friend called from San Francisco. A never-married man in his forties, Lee is trying to finish the Ph.D. he's wanted for years. It has taken perseverance and sacrifice. I told him about this section of the book, knowing that he had moved from Los Angeles because in San Francisco he could get by without "wheels." Never without his own car since high school, he moved and sold his late-model Buick. To quote Lee: "Tell them I dare them to try it. Once in a while I miss hopping into my car, but I surely don't miss the payments, the insurance, the maintenance, and the headaches!"

Spend as little as you can. "If I don't go skiing at least twice this winter I'll just die," I overheard someone say. I don't know where she hoped to ski, but as a recreational skier I do know that a hundred dollars per day for transportation, lodging, meals, and lift tickets is minimal (skis, boots, bindings, and ski clothes not included).

Some time ago I spoke at a national singles conference. The sponsors titled it "Traveling Light." Good idea. A primary principle of singling is to simplify your life, not to complicate it. Spending less will reap the same net result as earning more, and with less hassle. The key word in figuring out your budget is "need." We all have needs, but too easily convince ourselves that niceties are necessities.

Be starkly honest with yourself in separating your needs from your wants. Ultimately, our basic needs are clean air and water, reasonably nutritious food, shelter from the elements, and love.

You may conclude that you also need counseling, or to live by yourself. Fair enough; those could be wise investments. Some singlers feel a "need" for a vacation in Europe, a stereo system, or season tickets to the opera. Only you can determine how much you can afford to spend, and it would be folly to deprive yourself of everything you want. But prioritize your wants, and then stick with the priorities your means will allow.

Barter. Bartering is one way to spend less money. To barter is simply to exchange commodities or services rather than using money to purchase them. The barter system has always been a part of human society, and fortunately for singling individuals it is enjoying a resurgence. "Swap meets" are popular these days.

Bartering takes many forms. Ruth and Rochelle, both single mothers, regularly swap evenings or weekends of child care, and Ruth uses Rochelle's washer and dryer in exchange for Rochelle's occasional use of Ruth's van. You may not think you have much to offer for bartering purposes, but everyone has something. A physically handicapped businesswoman reads aloud to her blind neighbor in exchange for home-cooked suppers. The women's movement has especially encouraged bartering as a means of saving money and building a support system. In many cities networks of barterers have organized to publish directories. If you cannot find a barterers' network where you live, start one. All it takes is two singling people who can offer each other a personal service.

Since no money is exchanged, a helpful byproduct of bartering is that it may avoid taxes.[5]

Avoid taxes. I know a single woman, an executive secretary with no other income, who consistently pays more taxes than many doctors, lawyers, or business owners. To evade taxes is unlawful, but no one should pay more taxes than are absolutely required. To avoid unnecessary taxes is simply to refrain from throwing money away.

Tax laws, forms, and filing procedures have become increasingly complicated. For many singling people, hiring a tax accountant is worthwhile, especially if they don't enjoy tax math. Not only can skillful accountants save you more than their fees, but their fees are tax-deductible. Furthermore, they can furnish advice about tax-excluded or tax-deferred savings, information that can be very useful to singlers who are not homeowners.

Check your Social Security credits. As you begin singling, remember to send in a form postcard, available at all post offices and Social Security Administration offices, to request an updated report on your Social Security earnings. Such a report is your right, and you should ask for it every few years. If the Social Security Administration has made mistakes, it is far easier to correct them early than after many years have lapsed. Errors are common, especially when people change their surnames, as many women do.

Maintain adequate insurance. Judithann exemplified singlehood in many ways. She combined single parenting with a Ph.D. education and a very challenging career, and made it all fit. At the same time, she carried no insurance except on her automobile. When cancer surgery forced her to do hard thinking about her daughters' education and other needs should their mother die, she decided to buy life insurance. No carrier would write a policy on her because of the cancer.

Insurance is a drag to many singles. But what would happen if you became disabled? Are you adequately protected against illness, fire, burglary, accidents, lawsuits? The need for protection varies from person to person. The trick is to find an insurance agent willing to help you with the coverage you truly need, without making you insurance-poor.

A couple of insurance ideas are particularly useful to singlers. First, ordinary life insurance in general, while good protection, is a poor investment. It is often better to buy term insurance, which is pure protection at far less cost than whole life with its cumulative savings feature. Then, invest the premium difference in a higher interest account.

Second, if you do own an ordinary life policy (many of us do, left over from college days or married years), it may be wise to cash in the policy or convert it to another kind of protection, or at least borrow its cash value and invest the cash. The insurance company must lend the money to you at the rate stated in the policy, often 5 percent or 6 percent. Current interest rates paid by credit unions and money market funds are much higher. You can reap the benefits of the difference rather than (in effect) subsidizing the insurance company.

Hire a financial adviser. If this discussion has been redundant and you could have written it better, you need no financial adviser or already have one. But you need a financial adviser if *(a)* you found this material boring, or *(b)* you don't have much money. Those of us who care little about money matters need help. The less money one has to spend, the more careful one must be. Someone with a six-figure income can gamble away several thousand dollars and have plenty left, but for most of us financial mistakes hurt.

A warning: Some people who call themselves financial advisers, estate planners, or personal money managers actually are not; their expertise is in sales. They sell tax shelters, land investments, securities, second trust deeds, or commodities—on a commission basis. It is scarcely possible for one who has products to sell, and whose livelihood depends on sales commissions, to keep your best interests at heart.

Good financial advisers have nothing to sell except time and advice, usually at an hourly rate. Some are lawyers, CPAs, MBAs, or former business executives, but not all. Increasingly the credential to look for is C.F.P. (Certified Financial Planner), a "ticket" requiring specific training and stiff exams covering all aspects of the field.

Even more important, find someone recommended by friends or colleagues, and then ask for references and check them out. In what specific ways has this person helped clients? Have they ever gotten a "bum steer" from the planner? Has the planner personally sold them anything? (If so, beware.) Does the planner specify what the client should do with money, or instead point out possibilities and make the client choose? Ethical financial advisers do the latter.

Living Alone

By choosing to live alone we may think we are avoiding pressures, but sometimes it's not that simple. Robin tells his story:

> I want to become single, and I like your idea of "singling" because it means I don't have to do it all overnight. I can

go at my own speed. I need that, because I'm thorough, but I'm slow. As you know, I'm in therapy and also living alone. Both are things I never dreamed of doing, but here I am. I'm proud of myself because I got awfully lonely and depressed after my divorce. But I'm all right now.

I'm a conformist, not a rebel, and I find it distressing that to some people living alone is an act of rebellion. I didn't expect to cause such a fuss. My parents had a fit because I'm spending seven hundred dollars a month on an apartment for just me. They asked how much my rent was, so I told them. I should have lied. I don't dare tell them my utility costs or what I spend eating out several nights a week.

They told me to move in with some nice family as a roomer and save my money to invest in a fourplex. (INTERVIEWER: A fourplex?) Yeah, you know, be a landlord, not a tenant. But I just can't. Not right now.

Even my friends are on my case. One of them just asked to move in with me. After all, we could do stuff together and save money too. He had a fit when I said no. He just couldn't see that it's not about him at all; it's all about me. I need to be alone.

Living alone is difficult. The first problem singling people encounter when they face the possibility of living alone is summed up in the memorable line of a comic-strip character, Walt Kelly's Pogo: "We have met the enemy and he is us." As Pogo's line implies, people sabotage themselves. A never-married man called Tom, living alone for the first time, said it during a counseling session:

I've become so brainwashed that I honestly feel there's something wrong with me for liking my own company so well. I actually feel selfish or tainted for so thoroughly enjoying a sunset or a symphony alone. I look back over my own shoulder and wonder: Ought not I to be sharing this with someone?

Robin's story implied a second difficulty: The impact of the surrounding culture is enormous. One singling adult said, "I'm not especially concerned about having no plans for a special dinner on my birthday—but my mother sure is!"

Note the words of Tom again, later in the same interview:

> The other morning I woke up feeling good, at peace with myself. I was alone and happy. I enjoyed my coffee and the newspaper. I left for work calm, cool, and collected. By the end of the day I felt so bombarded by the togetherness messages on billboards, radio, and TV, images of everybody doing everything in groups—not to mention the couples I saw holding hands on the street—that I came home lonely. Well, not genuinely lonely; more as if I thought I was supposed to feel lonely. I was thinking: If I'm not lonely, what's wrong with me?

The world will disturb our peace if we allow it, especially when we are trying to hear the beat of a different drummer. The lyrics of popular songs, our American folk "hymnody," constantly push us to embrace non-singleness. I call these "no-growth songs for non-singles." Listen for them. Don't just enjoy the tune or beat; listen to the words. Whether you prefer jazz, country and Western, "easy listening" music, or rock, with practice you will become acutely aware of lyrics you never noticed before—insistent lyrics preaching that one's happiness is utterly dependent on giving one's power away to another person!

A third problem is that most would-be singles are still non-single in their hearts, in at least one big way: They are addicted to the notion of romantic love.

Up to the thirteenth century or so, the idea of romantic love was left to poets and minstrels. People got married or did not, but if they did it was for economic, religious, and childbearing purposes. Typically, love became part of a relationship only later, if at all, as in many world cultures today.

Only during recent centuries has love in its sentimentalized form come to be viewed as the necessity for "normal" living. It is as if the poetic utterances of early troubadors have been canonized and lent an air of desperation.

So, as sophisticated and wise as today's would-be singles are, and as much as they think singling is a terrific idea, many still harbor in their hearts the fervent dream that someday, somehow, Mr. or Miss or Ms. Right will come along and lift their burden of lonesomeness, turn their night into day, fill their eyes with tears of joy and their ears with whispers of sweet nothings, create instant passion day or night, and with peace and comfort lead them hand in hand into paradise. If the statement seems melodramatic, it is how many so-called singles actually feel. For all their facade of street-smart worldliness, their hearts belong to Victorian tradition.

A fourth difficulty is: Living alone is expensive. Often one's singling time is a time when one can barely afford necessities, and living alone may be a luxury beyond reach. House or apartment sharing may be the best alternative. Spaces can be shared without sharing relationships or lifestyles. But see to it that the contract is clear from the start. All parties need to understand that you will be "living alone together."

Living alone is valuable. Living alone is hardly the only choice singling adults can make. But ask yourself not only, "Can I afford to live alone?" but also, "Can I afford *not* to live alone?" Here are five ideas to consider before you answer the question:

First, living by yourself can help you *learn to celebrate your aloneness.* As a singling person, a most helpful step along the path is discovering individually the unadorned beauty of who you are. It is to celebrate your child-of-Godness, femaleness, maleness, blackness, whiteness, shortness, tallness, elderliness, youthfulness, whatever—just who and what you are or, as one woman put it, "who and what God intended when God made me." To do this is first to face and celebrate the fact that you are alone—which means also to celebrate the fact that you are free. As a singling pioneer, you can be a change maker in the lives of others. But first you must celebrate your own aloneness. Living alone can help you learn how.

Second, living alone can help you *become well married to yourself.* To be alone and to master that aloneness is an enormous task. It is the task of learning to know yourself, love yourself, have mercy on yourself, be kind and gentle to yourself, laugh at yourself, forgive yourself, desentimentalize your view of yourself, and be more and more self-supporting. In short, it is learning to be your own best friend.

One can be well married to oneself. One can learn to sort out her or his own foibles and limitations from others' imperfections and the difficulties that come with living in a flawed world. One can learn to take responsibility for one's personal health and wholeness. One can learn to use one's freedom to make choices, wholesome choices about how to live and with (or without) whom. One can learn to be wary of the seductions of needy persons who treat themselves like garbage while imploring others to treat them like diamonds. Indeed, for one who wants to be prepared for the possibility of a committed primary relationship, the most important condition for being well married to another person is first to be well married to oneself. One good way to achieve that state of personal wellness is through the learnings that come from living alone.

Living alone can also facilitate relating to others, for unless at some time and place in our lives we experience aloneness (and loneliness) for what it is, unless we learn to be creative and make ourselves whole, we humans have relatively little to bring to other persons when we do love them. Instead all we bring is our own needs, demands, passions, fears, jealousies, and well-intentioned but confused gestures. So becoming well married to yourself is an important singling task.

There are many practical ways in which living alone can help you become well married to yourself. Among them:

1. *You can manage your personal time the way you want.* Read away a rainy weekend. Be a night person. Be a morning person. "Pig out" on TV or movies. Jog or walk instead of eating at the usual time.
2. *You can eat the way you want.* A reporter asked a famous single woman's daughter, "Is your mother a good cook?" Her reply: "My mother doesn't cook; she thaws." Of course, nutrition is a concern. Here are some ideas:
   - Buy small. It is worth a quick stop on the way home. Fruits and vegetables are inexpensive, nutritious, and best when fresh.

- A vegetable steamer, which inserts into any saucepan, is a good investment.
- A slow cooker (Crockpot) with a timing device can be set up to have dinner ready when you come home.
- Frozen foods have come a long way. Quality is now available in individual portions. Preparation is efficient and quick, using either cooking pouches or a microwave oven.
- Use take-outs (Chinese, Italian, for example) for convenience and a change of pace. Ethnic foods are generally more nutritious than "fast food" take-outs.
- Delicatessens offer individual portions of a wide variety of quality meats, cheeses, ready-to-eat pastas, and salads.
- Most restaurants charge much less at noon than at night—sometimes for virtually the same food. If you eat dinner out at noon several times a week, you can fix a simple meal like lunch on those evenings at home.

3. *You can keep house the way you want.* All the "common space" is yours! Put your piles where you want them. Be as neat and clean as you wish, or keep your entertainment space presentable and other rooms messy. It's up to you. Hire someone for the heavy seasonal housework, or have a housekeeper come in for a half day twice a month. Another work saver is to use a wash/dry/fold or "bachelor bundle" service instead of doing laundry yourself. This leads to the next advantage of living alone.
4. *You can spend your money the way you want.* Budget carefully or don't follow a budget at all—it's your choice. If you hate paying bills and are apt to be delinquent, I know of two solutions. One is to pay bills the very day you receive them, even if it means strapping yourself financially or postdating checks and carrying them around for a while. The other is to hire someone to keep your records and pay your bills. For those who can afford it, this is a nice service, though it is a luxury unless one has a big income.
5. *You can avoid traps that commonly snare singlers.* These include getting caught up in a housemate's problems,

sharing a lifestyle you would not choose, or becoming the object of jealousy when things go well for you. You may even avoid "falling in love" with the wrong person just because you hate your living situation and want to escape it.

A third idea to consider, if you have preadult children, is that *living alone can help you with single parenting.* One can live alone and be a good parent. It is simpler, of course, if you are not the sole or primary custodial parent. It is a singles' boon that joint custody is now quite common. But even if you are your children's only parent, a home for you and your children is far more conducive to singling than a home for you and your children plus your mother, sibling, or lover.

Sociologist Robert Weiss, a leading authority on single parenting, reports that the singling custodial parents he studied reported positive benefits to living alone with their children. Weiss's subjects said that *(a)* it's better than living in a bad marriage; *(b)* it's nice to be able to decide things for oneself; *(c)* one comes to think better of oneself; and *(d)* one builds a special relationship with one's children.[6] On the down side, they also spoke of insufficient support, responsibility overload, task overload, and emotional overload.[7] Adding people to your household will heighten these burdens, however, not ease them.

Even in an extreme case, where your parental duties are unavoidable and yours alone—let's say you are a widow with small children—you need "alone time" and "alone space" for all the reasons mentioned here. Do yourself the favor of living as alone as you can. Try to arrange care for your children occasionally outside of your home so you can be home by yourself, preferably overnight. The rest of the time commandeer a space in your home that is yours alone—a room, attic, or cubbyhole "off limits" to anyone but you—and make time to use it.

By all means, place your personal singling needs atop your priority list! Many singling mothers programmed to deny their own needs for the sake of their children feel guilty because they work outside the home. Please note: *(a)* There is no evidence based on research that children with working mothers grow up inferior; and *(b)* children with a non-single mother who is "married to the kids" will become non-single adults.

A fourth, sobering idea is: This may be *your only chance to live alone.* You will recall that no one starts life single; singling must be done intentionally. Your time of singling may not only be the best time to live alone; it may be the only time. Many who read this will marry. The statistics favor it, and often when one no longer needs a thing to happen, it does. If you do marry, I hope you will marry knowing how to live alone successfully.

Non-singles are people who may not know how to live together but can't stand living apart. Mature singles have a choice, because they know how to do both—live together or live solo.

When Daisy's contractor husband died, leaving her widowed at age seventy, she took time to grieve but then, two years later, she sold the large home she called "the house that George built" and moved to a small condominium. Asked why, she said:

> I couldn't live alone in the house that George built. For one thing, it was too much house for me to manage without constant helpers around. But more than that, George was everywhere in that house. He not only built it, he designed it with help from an architect friend. His thumbprint was in every nook and cranny. Now I want to live alone. My new place will have only *my* thumbprint. I want to do it while I can. Luckily, I was able to sell the house that George built for ten times the cost of building it.

And fortunately Daisy was well enough to take care of herself as a septuagenarian. She lived alone in her condo for several years and became a world traveler. Now Daisy is an octogenarian and lives in a community for elders. She is well, happy, and glad she took advantage of her chance to live alone.

Fifth, living alone now *will help you later.* Like Daisy, many people as they grow older can no longer live alone because their physical health won't permit it. Of course, when one considers the alternative to aging, aging is not a bad deal. Even now, Daisy continues to enjoy life to the full. People like her, who know how to make the best of a difficult situation, will make the best of their next difficult situation too. So even if you are half Daisy's age, living alone now will help you later.

I must admit that I have never yet mastered aloneness for any prolonged period. I am an extroverted person energized by interactions with other people, and I seem to have batteries that crave that energy. In spite of that, I strongly favor a period of living alone because it helped me so much. Living alone for the first time ever during my late thirties and early forties, I grew in my own self-support skills, which included the ability to be my own friend, contentedly alone.

Living alone is possible. The very thought of living alone, however, frightens some people, even if they can manage it financially. Here, then, is a "singler's survival kit" to use as you begin living alone.

1. *Be particular about your work environment.* If your workplace is a happy, peaceful setting where you are surrounded by people you enjoy, or if your career is something you would do without pay if you were independently wealthy, living alone will be relatively easy. If your workplace is lonesome or stressful or you hate your job, living alone will be more difficult.

If you need to change jobs, buy a copy of *What Color Is Your Parachute?* and follow its advice, or find a career counselor. *Parachute* will teach you how.[8]

2. *Learn to deal with restaurants, movies, and concerts by yourself.* There are advantages to being a party of one. Because the entertainment world tends to come packaged for two, you can almost always get a single ticket to a play, opera, concert, or ballet. I purchased a single front-row-center seat twenty minutes before a sold-out performance. A gourmet dinner before or after the theater can add pleasure to your evening.

Be aware that some restaurants tend to mistreat singles, especially single women, by ushering them to an undesirable table near the kitchen. It is important to have assertion skills (see chapter 11). You may feel less conspicuous by avoiding weekend nights, when hordes of twosomes go out on the town.

3. *Learn to give yourself presents.* Ursula, as she began living

alone after her husband's death, wisely asked herself, "What would Dean have given me for my birthday?" . . . and gave it to herself. You needn't have a great deal of money or be a widow to adopt this practice. Reward yourself for a job well done, or simply for living alone for a year (or a month!).

4. *Plan exciting vacations.* A friend of mine who lives alone calls hers "semispectacular" vacations. She has a modest income, yet she has taken Caribbean cruises and traveled in Europe, sometimes by herself, sometimes with a friend. She seems to always have a semispectacular vacation to look forward to.

5. *Volunteer for something you believe in.* Sing in a choir; become a Scout leader; give time to viewer-supported television; participate in a social-justice project for a cause such as world hunger, Habitat for Humanity, or refugee resettlement. Participate in the singles organization in your synagogue or church. Join Big Brothers/Sisters of America. Suicide prevention centers and other "hot line" organizations always need volunteers; most of them offer excellent crisis intervention and assertiveness training as a generous bonus.

6. *Splurge on telephone calls.* When living alone, your telephone can be a lifeline. So is the mail, but the phone is more immediate. Cultivate it as an ally. Long-distance calls are cheap at certain times, and telephone companies will help you get the most for your telephone dollar if you ask them.

7. *Purposefully reach out to people.* Find a car pool instead of commuting to work alone. Ask for hugs from people you trust. Take regular walks in your neighborhood. Find folks with interests or hobbies similar to yours. Do some "friendwork." (Review chapter 9, "Friendship and Singling.")

If you are introverted or shy, don't just hibernate on weekends, holidays, or in the wintertime. Hibernation leads to overwhelming feelings of lonesomeness or depression. If, on the other hand, you are extroverted and socially active, don't spread yourself thin in a flurry of activity. Through hyperactivity you may avoid *being* alone even though you live alone.

In sum, a year or two of living alone can help you in many kinds of ways. Consider it.

13

Marriage as a Singling Activity

It is appropriate for a book about singling to conclude with some words about coupling. Many who read this book will marry, some for the first time, some once again.

One hopes they will take whatever time they need to become fully single, well married to themselves, first. Here is a paradox: The more single one becomes, the less one needs marriage; the less one needs marriage, the more one is free to marry; the more one is free to marry, the less one seeks marriage; the less one seeks marriage, the more marriage seeks one.

I believe in marriage. It can be as legitimate a lifestyle as singlehood. Remembering that singlehood is not a state defined by law but a condition of existence, marriage is also a condition of existence. The two, singlehood and marriage, can coexist in the same persons, and married is an all right way to live life *once you are truly single.* It is an all wrong way to live life if you are still non-single, because it renders singling very difficult, perhaps impossible. Usually the result is a neurotic marriage between two non-singles, or a brief marriage between two people wishing they were single, or a messy marriage between a single person and a non-single one.

Three additional ideas will introduce our discussion of marriage as a singling activity.

First, I do not confine the term "marriage" to traditional marriages with a wedding ceremony, gold rings, and a legal document. I use the term generically to include all relationships usually characterized by committed coupling, exclusivity in sexual matters, and a pooling of finances and other resources.

Even in churchly circles it is now widely held that marriage is primarily a spiritual union and, as such, impossible to preserve by form, force, law, or doctrine. To put it another way, religious authorities agree that love as evidenced by faithful behavior is requisite to the establishing and sustaining of a spiritual unity that may properly be described as marriage. It follows, then, that a "dead marriage" is functionally as broken as one in which one of the spouses has physically died.

My concern here is with "live marriages"—spiritual unions based on love as evidenced by faithful action. I am not arguing against the value of the legal or religious aspects of institutional marriage. I do, however, harbor dreams for the institution. For one thing, I'd like it to become at least as difficult to get a marriage license as it is to get a driver's license. For our purposes, however, I leave these matters to the legislators and theologians.

Second, I am not arguing in favor of marriage. If anything, I am arguing against it because it serves many people poorly. I certainly am arguing against premature or inappropriate marriage. In effect, in this chapter I am saying *(a)* avoid marriage if you can, *(b)* make sure you are fully single before you contemplate marriage, and *(c)* if you do decide to marry, do it with eyes wide open.

Third, there are alternatives to traditional marriage. While our culture presently has only one kind of sanctioned marriage, namely monogamy or "closed" marriage, alternatives seem to be constantly emerging and evolving: two-couple marriages; "corporate" marriages between an indeterminate number of persons who merge their families and create a nonprofit corporation; short-term "contract" marriages; various forms of so-called "open" marriage where two people have a primary relationship and certain values to which each is committed, while various aspects of everyday living are negotiable; and so forth.

Let me speak plainly. I am not at all convinced that any of these alternatives is an improvement over traditional marriage, but the clearer you are about what marriage means for you and what you want from it, the more likely you are to approximate your goal. At the very least, if you have done your homework, you can negotiate with conviction from an intelligent position.

What Truly Single People Bring to Marriage

Since marriage is at best an "even odds" gamble, one ought not to contemplate it without at least three kinds of singling skills. I base these observations on several healthy marriages I know—marriages between persons who were fully single first.

First, persons who combine healthy singlehood with a healthy marriage are *highly skilled at negotiating without becoming defensive,* even in a relationship with a great deal at stake. Healthily married singles are like those rare couples who are successful business partners. They bring to each other the ability to solve problems as they arise, the ability to handle feelings (especially hostile feelings), the ability to negotiate issues related to power and control, and the ability to define and redefine roles as needed. When it works, such a partnership is beautiful to watch.

If you don't know how to fight—fair but firm, merciful but just, malleable but tough and resilient, knowing when to give ground but also when to hold your ground—you are not ready for marriage. Of course, you might marry a weak, not-so-bright non-single person you can easily dominate, but having come this far you wouldn't do that.

Second, well-married singles are *no longer haunted by the ghosts of yesteryear.* The partners do not dump hurtful, blameful garbage on their mates—refuse that belongs, if it belongs anywhere, on ex-spouses, mothers, fathers, or employers. On the contrary, these are people who are well married to each other because long ago they divorced their respective parents and former spouses emotionally and became well married to themselves. They do not need to fight their way out of their original families or former mating relationships. They do not need to use their mate as the nearest object on which to project their unfinished business.

Some of these good marriages between singles, incidentally, are second or third marriages, and I know one that is a fourth. But whether the earlier relationships ended by death, desertion, or divorce, the present partners have made peace with past relationships. A rule of thumb suggests itself as a test of whether you are ready for a new mating commitment: If you cannot tolerate the presence of an ex-lover or ex-spouse—whether by letter, photo, telephone, or face-to-face—you have not yet emotionally separated from that person. And if your intended mate cannot tolerate the presence of your ex-lover or ex-spouse—let's say at your wedding ceremony, or a party, or a lunch date "for old times' sake"—you have made a premature choice. More marriages are undermined and destroyed by this one dynamic, possessiveness, than by any other. Possessiveness is a profoundly non-single attribute. If you've forgotten what it looks like or how it feels, spend half a day with an infant or toddler as a reminder.

Finally, healthy singles' marriages have in common one other major ingredient, namely *mutualities.* As with good friendships, their relationships have a "1 + 1 = 1 + 1 + 1" or "third self" quality.[1] A healthily single person will not marry anyone he or she would not choose as a friend.

A "married singles" couple I know exemplifies this well. They have similar personal values, compatible work values, comparable intellectual capacities, and a common religious commitment. Both are intense persons, sexually attracted to each other, and respectful of each other's talents and skills. She earns more money than he, and that's OK with them both. He is more domestically oriented than she, and that's also OK with them both. They bear witness to the fact that with a high degree of mutuality two people can sustain a high level of mutual need satisfaction.

One of the finest masters of mutuality I ever met wrote:

> Without mutual willingness of me as a self to affirm you as a self, no meeting is possible—no encounter, no loving. And until there is mutuality in our attempts to encounter one another, I alone (or you alone) can do nothing to make "meeting" happen. In other words, loving/meeting happens within the context of mutuality or not at all.[2]

To put it simply: If you have not mastered mutuality, the art of loving encounter, you are not ready for marriage.

The best place to master mutuality is in a long friendship. It can also be done in a long courtship—the kind of evolution some marrieds experience when they marry very young and "grow up together."

In adulthood, mutualities must be brought into a marriage if the marriage is to have them at all. Non-singles strongly tend to seek "complementary" mates—people who are opposites, who have what they lack within themselves. True singles who decide to marry, on the other hand, strongly tend to seek "symmetrical" mates—people who have what they already have in abundance. Good marriages have many mutualities from the start.

What Marriage Does Poorly or Not at All

There are some things people often hope marriage will bring, which it cannot produce. Among the things we should not expect:

Marriage is a poor substitute for a cure. Anything needing curing that is the basis for a marriage promptly infects the marriage. Count on it: If you marry Susie or Pete to help you cure quirks, idiosyncrasies, habit patterns, and prejudices you spent a lifetime accumulating, you will be disappointed. You are far more apt to contaminate your mate than to get cured. One wag defined marriage as two people dedicating their neuroses to each other. The wag who gave this irreverent definition is a renowned marriage counselor.

Second, *marriage is a poor environment for personal growth.* A good marriage might add to one's feeling of self-worth *if* one enters it feeling worthful in the first place. But the love of a spouse can never compensate for the love one failed to get as a child. Marriage is like a garden that requires constant tending lest it return to the wild. Its soil is more apt to grow weeds of neglect than roses of content. Its water is more apt to rain on one's parade than to quench one's thirst. Its air is more apt to stifle individuation (singling) than to encourage it.

Countless people approach therapists complaining of the inadequacy of their spouse's love when no amount of spousal love would be enough to fill their emptiness. Others come to therapy feeling smothered by their spouse's insecurity or possessiveness, yet in their own insecurity they cling to the very ties that bind them. If personal blossoming is needed, marriage makes a poor nursery.

Third, *marriage offers no guarantee of a faithful or permanent partner.* We live in a society of serial marriage, a sort of sequential polygamy wherein the average length of marriages is a mere seven years and extramarital affairs abound. Marriages that last longer are becoming unusual, and many long marriages endure more because of inertia or fear than because of excitement or devotion. American spouses don't come with a "till death us do part" guarantee anymore. The reason is simple. They are enlightened humans living to very ripe old ages in a highly unpredictable world. If you need a "till death us do part" guarantee, a set of wrenches or some cookware is a safer bet. If you want a non-single female partner you might move to a Third World developing nation where women are still enslaved in second-class citizenry, but then you'll have to live in fear that your new homeland might develop. If you want a non-single male partner, you have the better of it; there are still plenty of non-single men to go around right here in the good old U.S.A.

What Marriage Does Rather Well

Marriage can offer two singles some worthwhile benefits under favorable circumstances, and a wise single will surely not marry unless the circumstances are indeed favorable. For your consideration, here are five possibilities.

First, *marriage is a good rock-polishing device.* The efficient way to polish rocks is to tumble them together, usually with some water and sand. In due time they knock the rough edges off each other and both become smooth and more beautiful, allowing the colors of each to shine. Rocks of approximately equal size and density work best.

Of course, while people may be as hard as rocks, they are not rocks. Tumbling can hurt and make one dizzy and angry. We resist being stripped of our defensive armor and getting our naked vulnerabilities polished. However, we all carry within us an inevitable tension between our thrusts toward autonomy and our pull toward relatedness, so that while we were singling we may have developed an acute longing for "tumbling."

A close friendship is a good rock-polishing device too, but friendships tend to be intermittent—a few hours per week at the most. Marriage can be the better rock-polishing device because of its intensity and continuity. Do find an equal rock, however, and prepare yourself for an abrasive good time. As one couple put it, "We married singles are lovingly brutal with each other."

Second, *marriage is a good arena for practicing commitment.* Making a commitment and honoring it no matter what seems to build character and depth. The people I admire most, those who have challenged me toward excellence most, have been masters of commitment.

One of them was Erik, my college professor. For many years Erik remained committed and faithful to his wife while she lay comatose in a state of limbo from which she was never to recover. He cared for her (with help) in their home, reared his children, taught brilliantly, and found time to befriend his students. Erik and I kept in touch until after she died and he remarried. I often marveled that anyone could sustain the level and length of faithfulness I saw in Erik. I have personally observed such commitment only in relation to a spouse.

A word of caution. Unless you marry an orphan with no family at all, you commit yourself and your marriage to relate to three family systems: the unique new nuclear family system created by your marriage and its children and any stepchildren, pets, neighborhood, home environment, and friendship network; your own original family's system; and your spouse's family system.

Be prepared to give more than you receive. As an investment marriage-related commitments make little sense—the rate of interest is too low. The commitments get complicated, tedious, costly, and dreadfully time-consuming as holiday seasons, birthdays and anniversaries, deaths and wakes, good times and bad come and go and come and go again, offering occasional joys and incessant obligations.

Lest I sound cynical, there may come a time when a person

(even a fully single one) decides the opportunity for commitment and possibility of becoming part of three families is worth whatever it costs.

Third, *marriage provides a good arena for building a history.* Bearing and rearing children, building an estate, tending a family tree and watching it bear fruit—these can provide a joyous sense of continuity and accomplishment over time. When a marriage breaks, this sense is one of the features most missed. Divorcing people will say, "I mourn the loss of what we've built together," or "I feel as though I've not just lost a spouse; I've lost a family and a history."

Fourth, *marriage is a good base camp from which to climb certain mountains.* I celebrate the fact that one can today bear or adopt children as a single. However, child-rearing is truly easier in a marriage with committed co-parents. So is home ownership. A hideaway in the mountains or at the beach, a nest egg for later, or spare cash for world travel—all may be easier to come by as a married single than going it alone. (Keep in mind that if the marriage breaks all gains are lost, and more.)

Changing careers can sometimes be easier married than unmarried. Many a person has been enabled to start a business or complete an advanced degree because of the security of a spouse's ongoing income and emotional support. The danger, of course, is that a career change can upset a marriage's delicate balance. In a recent study at one graduate school, 75 percent of the married students who began a doctoral program were no longer married by the time they received their Ph.D. degrees.

Fifth, *marriage is a good laboratory for learning humility.* A marriage in today's world is freighted with such awesome difficulty, and life as one autonomous single committed to living with another autonomous single can be so challenging, that it can be sustained only in a spirit of true humility. It demands total exposure of one's warts and flaws, utter vulnerability to hurt or even betrayal, and full awareness of one's limitations. If this is what you want as a fully single adult, go for it and Godspeed. But there are easier pathways to humility.

To Hunt or Not to Hunt

Is it worth engaging in the hunt for someone to marry? You alone can decide whether to hunt and if so, how, when, where, and what amount of energy to devote to hunting. Many singles, including some of the wisest, have chosen *not* to engage in the hunt at all. Some of them are now married, others aren't. All of them are still single. As far as I can tell, neither group is happier than the other, and all of them are quite happy they decided not to go ahunting.

My own bias is that in today's world, few people are single enough to marry well until midlife, and from midlife on, the hunt, per se, is more trouble than its worth. This applies particularly to women, given our unequal, sexist culture.

So what is a singling person to do?

Nurture satisfying friendships. Foster your career power. Improve your personal appearance and impact. Socialize as much and as freely as you want. Date all the worthwhile people you can. Take a long hot bath, or throw a temper tantrum, all by yourself for the sheer joy of it. Become fully single. Remain open and alert to all the possibilities. And if marriage is to find you, it will. If it does not find you, your finding someone to marry you is not apt to improve the quality of your life in any worthwhile way.

At least not in the long run. In the long run, single is the only way to fly. In the short run, too.

To Hunt or Not to Hunt

Epilogue

Liberation movements ultimately help free everyone, not just the direct beneficiaries. Black liberation helps liberate white people as well as blacks, gray liberation helps liberate the young as well as the old, gay liberation helps liberate heterosexuals, and women's liberation helps liberate men. Singles, when truly free, will help everyone's liberation.

All liberation movements have their songs—old, new, borrowed, or blue. The singles movement needs songs too. Songs help us make it through hard times. I hope we will create unique musical ways of symbolizing singles' freedom and power. I leave you with one person's attempt at such a symbol, the hymn "SingleGod." Add it to your repertoire and use it in your church or singles group.

Godspeed. May the wind be at your back, and may you have songs in the night.

SingleGod

Where is wholeness, God who made me?
With what purpose was I built?
Since all creatures come in two kinds,
Unpaired one kinds sometimes wilt.
God of Jeremiah, Magdalena,
Hear the longing of my soul.
Take me now in your control.

True, there are some benefits for singles:
Coming, going as I please;

Silence, solitude and peace, but
No "Gesundheit" when I sneeze.
God of oneness, God of twoness,
God of threeness, hear my plea.
God of mercy, hear my plea.

Lord of flesh, embodiment of Spirit,
You, too, liked a warm embrace.
Close to brothers, sisters, children,
You must know my empty space.
Jesus, Master, offering friendship,
Be here when my need is strong.
Stay close by me when the night is long.

If you mean for me a partner,
One with whom to share my days,
Let your providential leading
Guide us both in all our ways.
Perfect maker, loving giver,
While I'm doing all I can,
Give me light to see your plan.

God our Father, blessed Mother,
Single source of wheat and wine,
Mold my femaleness and maleness,
Balanced well by your design.
Bring my union, all-transforming;
Make your likeness known in me.
Take my life and set it free.[1]

Notes

Prologue

1. John R. Landgraf, *Creative Singlehood and Pastoral Care* (Philadelphia: Fortress Press, 1982).
2. Ibid., p. 52.

Chapter 1: The Case for Singling

1. The notion of movement in three dimensions—namely, moving *toward,* moving *away from,* or moving *against*—is the creation of Karen Horney (1885–1952). She first used it to describe intrapersonal dynamics and interpersonal relationships in *Our Inner Conflicts* (New York: W. W. Norton & Co., 1945).

Chapter 2: When Reality Hits

1. Freely abstracted from Norman Cousins, writing in *Human Options,* 1981 edition.

Chapter 3: Singling Because of Death

1. I have adapted certain ideas and illustrations from my book *Creative Singlehood and Pastoral Care* (Philadelphia: Fortress Press, 1982).
2. There are exceptions. For example, losing one's spouse through suicide usually results in embarrassment and a state of crisis. In such a case, the singling path may be more like that of a divorced or deserted person.

3. I borrow the term "good grief" from Granger E. Westberg, whose book *Good Grief* has helped many bereaved persons. See "For Further Reading"; publication information not given here appears in the annotated bibliography.

4. I am indebted to Howard W. Stone for his statement of these dynamics in *Suicide and Grief* (Philadelphia: Fortress Press, 1972). See also Wayne E. Oates, *Pastoral Care and Counseling in Grief and Separation* (Philadelphia: Fortress Press, 1981) for a more extended treatment of grief phenomena, including anticipatory grief.

5. There may be exceptions, for tax purposes or other reasons. Also, timing is important; some people move too quickly. However, if you feel trapped in your home, and as if you have no choice, it is wise to seek counsel to help you sort out the reasons why.

6. For an in-depth treatment see Edward V. Stein, *Guilt: Theory and Therapy* (Philadelphia: Westminster Press, 1968).

7. See Psalm 139:14. The entire psalm merits careful study. It contains many treasures for singlers.

Chapter 4: Singling Because of Divorce

1. This discussion on crisis is extrapolated from an article titled "The Crisis: A Dangerous Opportunity," published in February 1979 in *The Church, Prayer, and Holistic Health,* a newsletter of the Pastoral Counseling Service of the Los Angeles Baptist City Mission Society. Dr. Carroll J. Wright, then director of the Pastoral Counseling Service, wrote the original piece including the poetry. I have freely abstracted from his article, adding ideas of my own and removing sexist language.

Chapter 5: Singling Because of Delay

1. U.S. statistics reported in the *San Francisco Examiner,* February 2, 1986.

Chapter 6: Singling by Design

1. Charles V. Gerkin, *Crisis Experience in Modern Life* (Nashville: Abingdon Press, 1979), p. 323, italics mine. Gerkin teaches pastoral psychology at Candler School of Theology, Emory University, Atlanta.

2. Ibid., p. 330, italics mine.

3. First stanza of a poem written in 1833 by John Henry Newman. Later set to music, "Lead, Kindly Light" became the popular hymn still sung today. Newman's "kindly light" was the Judeo-Christian God.

4. The terms "safekeeping self" and "experimental self" and the descriptive chart are adapted from an original formulation by Dr. George Prince, chairperson of Synectics, Inc., 17 Dunster Street, Cambridge, Mass., and are used with his permission.

5. Freely adapted from Paula Ripple, F.S.P.A., *Walking with Loneliness,* pp. 20–21.

6. I thank the Rev. Margaret Ann Cowden for permitting me to use her ideas on friendship. Both here and at places in chapter 9 I have borrowed her thought, freely abstracted from an unpublished paper delivered at a singles conference in Topeka, Kansas, in 1980. Ms. Cowden is Associate Executive Director of the Ministers and Missionaries Benefit Board of the American Baptist Churches, U.S.A.

Chapter 7: Anger and Singling

1. See "For Further Reading" for books on anger, assertiveness, and related topics, including grief.

2. Assertiveness (or assertion) training courses, workshops, or ongoing groups are available through community colleges, women's organizations, private and public mental health centers, churches, and so forth. Ask your friends, or be assertive by placing your name on various mailing lists of institutions that periodically conduct such training.

3. I am indebted to Dr. Frank W. Kimper for the substance of this model. With minor alterations the third, fourth, and fifth steps are his formulation.

4. W. W. Broadbent, *How to Be Loved,* conveys the spirit of this statement. His book is an excellent primer on giving and receiving love.

Chapter 8: Men, Women, and Singling

1. Vignette excerpted from John R. Landgraf, *Creative Singlehood and Pastoral Care* (Philadelphia: Fortress Press, 1982), p. 33.

2. In some circles a reverse of the male double standard and sexism is currently in vogue, resulting in a diminishing of the self-esteem of singling men. For example, some feminists may imply that "women are good, men are bad." This overcompensation is unfortunate, but it does not change my point.

3. John R. Landgraf, "The Impact of Therapeutic Marital Separation on Spouses in Pastoral Marriage Counseling" (unpublished Ph.D. dis-

sertation, School of Theology at Claremont, Claremont, Calif., 1973); see especially pp. 108–112 and Appendices B and C.

4. I am indebted to Dr. James B. Nelson for some ideas in this section, garnered from an address he delivered at an annual meeting of the American Association of Pastoral Counselors in Minneapolis, circa 1986. See also his book *The Intimate Connection.*

5. See John Sanford's *The Invisible Partners.* Subtitled "How the Male and Female in Each of Us Affects Our Relationships," Sanford's is an excellent treatment.

6. Research findings have demonstrated that in the United States married women have a lower level of mental health than married men while single women have a higher one than single men. See Jessie Bernard, *The Future of Marriage* (New York: Bantam Books, 1972) for further discussion.

Chapter 9: Friendship and Singling

1. Sam Keen, *The Passionate Life,* p. 215.

2. Herb Goldberg, *The Hazards of Being Male,* pp. 126–127, italics mine.

3. Keen, op. cit., pp. 216–217.

4. Muriel James and Louis M. Savary, *The Heart of Friendship.*

5. "People," words by Bob Merrill, music by Jule Styne.

6. "A Little Help from My Friends," words and music by John Lennon and Paul McCartney.

7. James and Savary, *The Heart of Friendship,* p. 27.

8. "Bridge Over Troubled Water," words and music by Paul Simon.

9. The reading list contains suggestions. As a general text, I particularly recommend Robert Shelton's *Loving Relationships.*

10. Lillian Rubin, *Just Friends: The Role of Friendship in Our Lives.*

11. Goldberg, *The Hazards of Being Male.*

12. The story of Saul of Tarsus (Saint Paul) is in Acts of the Apostles in the New Testament.

Chapter 10: Sex and Singling

1. Those interested in celibacy should read Janie Gustafson's *Celibate Passion.* Her chapters on "Celibate Passion" and "Erotic Intimacy" are particularly worthwhile.

2. Because of his prominence, I have taken particular pains to change not only "Nathan's" name but also several details in his story.

3. Morton Hunt, *Sexual Behavior in the 1970s* (New York: Dell Books, 1974), p. 67.

4. Lewis R. Rambo, *The Divorcing Christian,* p. 74.
5. Ibid., p. 75.
6. June Singer, *Androgyny: Toward a New Theory of Sexuality* (Garden City, N.Y.: Doubleday & Co., Anchor Books, 1976), p. 299, italics mine.
7. Ibid., p. 305, italics mine.
8. The idea of three basic choices in moral decision-making was described first by Joseph Fletcher in the 1960s. Here, however, my discussion is freely adapted from Lester A. Kirkendall's unpublished paper "Morality for Twentieth Century Living" (Corvallis, Ore.: Department of Family Life, Oregon State University, no date given).
9. James B. Nelson, *Embodiment,* pp. 126–127.
10. Ibid., p. 129.
11. Karen Lebacqz, *"A Sexual Ethic for Singles,"* unpublished essay prepared for the Professional Ethics Group of the Center for Ethics and Social Policy, Graduate Theological Union, Berkeley, California. Her quote is from Stanley Hauerwas, *A Community of Character: Toward a Constructive Christian Social Ethic* (Notre Dame, Ind.: University of Notre Dame Press, 1981), p. 181. A later version of her essay was published in *Christian Century* (May 6, 1987, pp. 435–438), under the title "Appropriate Vulnerability: A Sexual Ethic for Singles."
12. Ibid.
13. Ibid., italics mine.
14. "The Love Relationship" is adapted from the "awareness process" in Gestalt therapy, as formulated by Frederick S. Perls, M.D., and interpreted to me by Frank W. Kimper, Ph.D.

Chapter 11: Where to Find Help

1. Clinical training is counseling under supervision over a period of time, which is the best way to learn how to be a helper. Trainees are audiotaped and videotaped and produce written verbatim records of interviews as well as case studies.
2. Ecclesiastical endorsement signifies the imprimatur of one's denomination or faith group. It indicates the judicatory body's trust of a practitioner's clinical skills and ethics.
3. Normally, practitioners will be active in at least the primary reference group for their main discipline. For psychiatrists, this is the American Psychiatric Association; for psychologists, the American Psychological Association; for pastoral counselors, the American Association of Pastoral Counselors; for marriage, family, and child counselors, the American Association for Marriage and Family Therapy. Clinical social

workers are often active in the last organization (AAMFT) as well as in the National Association of Social Workers.

4. Androgyny is explained in chapter 8.

5. For a fuller treatment, see my article "Dealing with the Religious Client in Pastoral Counseling" in *Journal of Pastoral Psychology,* vol. 1[2], winter 1987, pp. 51–59.

6. Some of these descriptions are in Lynn Huber's excellent article "Toward a Spirituality of Aging" in *Centering* (vol. IV, no. 2, summer 1987). In one sense, spiritual development is aging gracefully. Since singling is also a matter of aging gracefully, it can be viewed as one form of spiritual development.

7. The recovery of homeopathic medicine, the holistic health movement, and an increased emphasis on self-responsibility for the maintenance of one's own wellness are examples. Even in the realm of physical medicine, we learn that it is anything but a complete or exact science. Certainly physical medicine has made important scientific advances—antibiotics and surgery, to name two—but beyond antibiotics and surgery physicians remain severely limited in what they can do.

8. M. Scott Peck, *The Road Less Traveled* (New York: Simon & Schuster, 1978), p. 168.

Chapter 12. Lifestyle Issues

1. Matthew 10:34–39. The wording follows *An Inclusive-Language Lectionary, Readings for Year A,* rev. ed., copyright © 1986 Division of Education and Ministry, National Council of the Churches of Christ in the U.S.A., based on the Revised Standard Version of the Bible.

2. From an unpublished sermon manuscript. The preacher asked that she remain anonymous.

3. Begin by buying a current copy of *What Color Is Your Parachute?* by Richard N. Bolles (Berkeley, Calif.: Ten Speed Press). *Parachute* is revised and updated every year. It is both the best self-help manual for job-hunters and career changers and an excellent referral guide for those seeking professional career guidance.

4. Authors to look for include Sylvia Porter, Andrew Tobias, and Richard K. Rifenbark. Any bookstore or library has their books and many others. My personal library includes Sylvia Porter, *The New Money Book* (Garden City, N.Y.: Doubleday & Co., 1979); Richard K. Rifenbark, *How to Beat the Salary Trap* (New York: Avon Books, 1978); and Andrew Tobias, *The Only Investment Guide You'll Ever Need* (New York: Bantam Books, 1979). *Money* magazine, available at newstands, is also helpful.

5. The Internal Revenue Service has ruled that taxable transactions, such as trading tangible products or professional services at discounts, must be declared for income-tax purposes. When in doubt about the legality of bartering, consult your tax preparer or IRS office to make sure you stay within legal bounds.

6. Robert S. Weiss, *Going It Alone,* pp. 260–265.

7. Ibid., pp. 265f.

8. Bolles, *What Color Is Your Parachute?*

Chapter 13. Marriage as a Singling Activity

1. See chapter 9.

2. Frank W. Kimper, "Musings on the Nature of Healthy Relationships" (Claremont, Calif.: unpublished article, 1973).

Epilogue

1. "SingleGod," words copyright 1985 by Forster Freeman, used with his permission. The Rev. Dr. Freeman ministers to singles at First Congregational Church, Berkeley, California. A suggested tune is CWM RHONDDA (John Hughes, 1907), found in many hymnals under the title "God of Grace and God of Glory." Dr. Freeman wrote "SingleGod" as a project for a course titled "Understanding and Ministering to Singles," which I taught in the Graduate Theological Union in 1985.

For Further Reading

Astrachan, Anthony. *How Men Feel.* Garden City, N.Y.: Doubleday & Co., Anchor Books, 1986. Males respond to women's demands for equality and power; a look at men's emotions and behavior as they face the women's revolution.

Augsburger, David W. *Anger and Assertiveness in Pastoral Care.* Philadelphia: Fortress Press, 1979. A useful, understandable approach to the constructive use of anger.

———. *When Caring Is Not Enough: Resolving Conflicts Through Fair Fighting.* Scottdale, Pa.: Herald Press, 1983. Teaches exactly what the title implies.

Barbach, Lonnie. *For Yourself: The Fulfillment of Female Sexuality.* Garden City, N.Y.: Doubleday & Co., 1975. A practical guide for women who want to learn sexual self-care.

Baumli, Francis, ed. *Men Freeing Men: Exploding the Myth of the Traditional Male.* Jersey City, N.J.: New Atlantis Press, 1985. Useful articles for men who want to become androgynous.

Bloomfield, Harold H., Melba Colgrove, and Peter McWilliams. *How to Survive the Loss of a Love.* New York: Bantam Books, 1977. Bite-sized first-aid ideas to help facilitate grief.

Broadbent, W. W. *How to Be Loved.* Englewood Cliffs, N.J.: Prentice-Hall, 1976. An accessible book that helps the singling person learn to achieve a sense of belonging without possessive or defensive tactics.

Buscaglia, Leo. *Love.* Thorofare, N.J.: Charles B. Slack, 1972.

Caine, Lynn. *Widow.* New York: Bantam Books, 1975. A first-person account. Inspiring reading for both women and men who have lost a mate because of death.

Claremont de Castillejo, Irene. *Knowing Woman: A Feminine Psychology.* New York: Harper & Row, Colophon Books, 1974. Written with subtlety, lucidity, and balance from a Jungian viewpoint. Significant chapters include "The Animus—Friend or Foe?" and "The Older Woman."

Cowan, Connell, and Melvin Kinder. *Smart Women, Foolish Choices: Finding the Right Men, Avoiding the Wrong Ones.* New York: Signet Books, 1985. Helpful awareness-raising for heterosexual women hooked on marriage as the one way to fulfillment.

Druck, Ken. *The Secrets Men Keep: Breaking the Silence Barrier.* Garden City, N.Y.: Doubleday & Co., 1985. For men who want to learn to be self-revealing, and for women who want to learn about men.

Goldberg, Herb. *The Hazards of Being Male.* New York: Signet Books, 1977. A "male liberation" primer; his chapter "The Lost Art of Buddyship" is especially important.

———. *The New Male: From Self-Destruction to Self-Care.* New York: Signet Books, 1980. Good sequel to *The Hazards of Being Male,* but read *Hazards* first.

Graver, Jane. *Single but Not Alone.* St. Louis: Concordia Publishing House, 1983. Sixty-three pages of meditations for single Christian women. Helps foster peace with singleness.

Gustafson, Janie. *Celibate Passion.* San Francisco: Harper & Row, 1978. Written by a Roman Catholic sister; encourages women toward long-term singlehood with spirituality as a cornerstone.

Harayda, Janice. *The Joy of Being Single.* Garden City, N.Y.: Doubleday & Co., 1986. Lots of useful ideas from a never-married former editor of *Glamour* magazine.

Israel, Martin. *Living Alone: The Spiritual Dimension.* New York: Crossroad Publishing Co., 1983. Living alone as one entryway into the fulfilled life.

Jackson, Edgar N. *Understanding Loneliness.* Philadelphia: Fortress Press, 1980. The final work of a true sage, profound yet very readable. The "Creative Solitude" chapter is invaluable.

James, Muriel, and Louis M. Savary. *The Heart of Friendship.* New York: Harper & Row, 1979. A fine primer on friendship.

Johnson, Nancy Karo. *Alone and Beginning Again.* Valley Forge, Pa.: Judson Press, 1982. Special help for widowed women.

Keen, Sam. *The Passionate Life: Stages of Loving.* San Francisco: Harper & Row, 1983. A philosophical essay on love, sexuality, friendship, and society. Not easy, but provocative and eminently rewarding.

Krantzler, Mel. *Creative Divorce.* New York: Signet Books, 1975. The "nine emotional traps" section is very worthwhile.

Lerner, Harriet Goldhor. *The Dance of Anger: A Woman's Guide to Changing the Patterns of Intimate Relationships.* New York: Harper & Row, 1985. Useful for both women and men. How to understand and reduce anger in relationships.

LeShan, Lawrence. *How to Meditate.* New York: Bantam Books, 1975. The best beginner's book on the topic. Good for those who want to learn to be alone contentedly.

Miller, Jean B. *Toward a New Psychology of Women.* Boston: Beacon Press, 1977. A clear, concise awareness raiser for men as well as women.

Miller, Keith, and Andrea Wells Miller. *The Single Experience.* Waco, Tex.: Word Books, 1981. Wonderful encouragement for singlers with a conservative religious background.

Moustakas, Clark E. *Loneliness and Love.* Englewood Cliffs, N.J.: Prentice-Hall, 1972. "Bibliotherapy" for the reader blocking catharsis or living alone. The chapter "Loneliness and Solitude" merits many readings.

Muto, Susan Annette. *Celebrating the Single Life: A Spirituality for Single Persons in Today's World.* Garden City, N.Y.: Doubleday & Co., Image Books, 1985. How to live life as a seriously committed single who is spiritually grounded.

Natale, Samuel M. *Loneliness and Spiritual Growth.* Birmingham, Ala.: Religious Education Press, 1986. Brings together the pertinent research on loneliness and shows how loneliness can lead directly to personal and spiritual growth.

Nelson, James B. *Between Two Gardens: Reflections on Sexuality and Religious Experience.* New York: Pilgrim Press, 1983. Help for persons who have trouble reconciling sexuality with spirituality.

———. *Embodiment.* Minneapolis: Augsburg Publishing House, 1979. Sexuality issues are carefully set within a biblical context in this scholarly but sensitive and readable treatise in theological ethics.

———. *The Intimate Connection.* Philadelphia: Westminster Press, 1988. Particular help with relationships as well as male and female sexuality. Especially useful reading for men.

Norwood, Robin. *Women Who Love Too Much.* Los Angeles: Jeremy P. Tarcher, 1985. Help for women who cling to destructive relationships or settle for less than mutuality.

Peck, M. Scott. *The Road Less Traveled.* New York: Simon & Schuster, 1978. Peck's modern classic on love, values, and spiritual growth is a good text for singlers who want to become well married to themselves.

Rambo, Lewis R. *The Divorcing Christian.* Nashville: Abingdon Press, 1983. Addressed to those experiencing divorce-related pain because of a Christian upbringing. Compassionate yet candid and blatantly honest.

Ripple, Paula. *The Pain and the Possibility.* Notre Dame, Ind.: Ave Maria Press, 1978. Essential reading for divorced Catholics, this book will help all divorced persons heal.

———. *Walking with Loneliness.* Notre Dame, Ind.: Ave Maria Press, 1982. Challenges one to live positively with loneliness, "a demanding and ever-present companion."

Rubin, Lillian B. *Intimate Strangers.* New York: Harper & Row, 1983. The best available book to help midlife adults understand how men and women operate relationally.

———. *Just Friends: The Role of Friendship in Our Lives.* New York: Harper & Row, 1985. Simply superb.

Sanford, John A. *The Invisible Partners.* New York: Paulist Press, 1980. About the masculine and feminine in each of us. Important reading for singlers who want to become androgynous.

Schultz, Terri. *Bittersweet: Surviving and Growing from Loneliness.* New York: Thomas Y. Crowell Co., 1976. A candid, positive approach with enlightening discussions on friendship, sexuality, and living alone.

Shelton, Robert. *Loving Relationships: Self, Others, and God.* Elgin, Ill.: Brethren Press, 1987. A must for anyone who has difficulty loving.

Smedes, Lewis B. *Forgive and Forget: Healing the Hurts We Don't Deserve.* San Francisco: Harper & Row, 1984. Help for the healing of memories.

Vaughn, Joe, and Ron Klug. *New Life for Men.* Minneapolis: Augsburg Publishing House, 1984. Instructive reading for all men.

Weiss, Robert S. *Going It Alone.* New York: Basic Books, 1979. Simply the best book in print on single parenting.

Westberg, Granger E. *Good Grief.* Philadelphia: Fortress Press, 1962. A simple, forthright, and constructive little classic. Particularly helpful for suddenly singling persons.

Zilbergeld, Bernie. *Male Sexuality.* New York: Bantam Books, 1978. For men to understand themselves better sexually and women who want to understand male sexuality.

Zimbardo, Philip G. *Shyness.* Reading, Mass.: Addison-Wesley Publishing Co., 1977. The definitive word on shyness—what it is and what to do about it.